THE GERALD KRAAK ANTHOLOGY

Pride and Prejudice

THE GERALD KRAAK ANTHOLOGY:
AFRICAN PERSPECTIVES ON GENDER,
SOCIAL JUSTICE AND SEXUALITY

Pride and Prejudice

First published by Jacana Media (Pty) Ltd, in partnership
with The Other Foundation, in 2017

10 Orange Street
Sunnyside
Auckland Park 2092
South Africa
+2711 628 3200
www.jacana.co.za

© Jacana Media and The Other Foundation, 2017
© Individual stories, poems and photographs
rests with individual contributors
All rights reserved.

ISBN 978-1-4314-2518-1

Cover design by Shawn Paikin
Set in Stempel Garamond 10.5/16pt
Printed and bound by Creda Communications
Job no. 002981

See a complete list of Jacana titles at www.jacana.co.za

Contents

Foreword vii
Editor's note xi
Poached eggs *Farah Ahamed* 1
A place of greater safety *Beyers de Vos* .14
Dean's bed *Dean Hutton* 40
Midnight in Lusikisiki or (The ruin of the gentlewomen)
    Sindiswa Busuku-Mathese 50
Two weddings for Amoit *Dilman Dila* .52
Albus *Justin Dingwall* 76
Resurrection *Tania Haberland* 88
For men who care *Amatesiro Dore* 89
Intertwined odyssey *Julia Hango* 97
You sing of a longing *Otosirieze Obi-Young* 106
The conversation *Olakunle Ologunro* 134
Stranger in familiar land *Sarah Waiswa* 145
One more nation bound in freedom *Ayodele Sogunro* 154
Biographies 164

Foreword

SETTLING ON AN appropriate way to honour the legacy of The Other Foundation's founding figure, Gerald Kraak, was a tough task. Gerald was, in so many ways, an enigma. We hope that *The Gerald Kraak Anthology: African Perspectives on Gender, Social Justice and Sexuality* will aptly capture his enigmatic character.

The anthology intends to depict the contradictions of contemporary Africa's progress in struggles for equality, freedom and social inclusion by gender-non-conforming people, yet it also aims to show the deep despair of hidden suffering. It wants to expose the paradox of new generations yearning for personal freedom and transcendence, yet it also wishes to display it in a historical mould of widely shared deprivation. It seeks to unmask the beauty of resilience in a stand for dignity – the same as generations displayed in struggles before.

The anthology was born of the determination of Gerald's close friend and collaborator, Carla Sutherland, who was the head of programmes at The Other Foundation. She convinced Martin O'Brien, vice president of The Atlantic Philanthropies, that the publication of this anthology would help to propel the construction of an African narrative of social justice for increasingly impatient homosexual and gender-non-conforming people.

We are very grateful for The Atlantic Philanthropies' generous investment in the publication of the anthology for five years.

This inaugural *Pride and Prejudice* volume carries the authoritative mark of the involvement of three of Africa's most appealing social justice and literary appraisers: Sisonke Msimang, Sylvia Tamale and Eusebius McKaiser. They worked through 393 entries from 20 countries across the continent to curate the finest depictions of Africa's contemporary commentaries on gender, social justice and sexuality.

Jacana Media and the Jacana Literary Foundation have been brilliant partners in bringing this project to life – with grace and such great competence. The project would hardly have moved forward at all without the firm commitment of Bridget Impey and Klara Skinner to make it succeed.

In setting up this award and planning for the anthology it was essential to explore and connect with partner publishers in Africa. In a tremendous show of support we received the enthusiastic approval and commitment from some of the most adventurous publishers on the continent and around the globe. The following publishers are all linked to the project, and their support in reaching out to writers has meant a great deal to the success and range of this anthology.

- Africa World Press, America
- Amalion, Senegal
- Femrite, Uganda
- Gadson Books, Zambia
- Kwani Trust, Kenya
- Sub-Saharan Publishers, Ghana
- Wordweaver Publishing house, Namibia

For now the political challenges in countries like Zimbabwe, Uganda and Ghana mean that some publishers can only join us in spirit, for others the economic realities of publishing in Africa leave them with little means to print and distribute in their countries.

The Other Foundation is a community foundation for homosexual and bisexual women and men, and transgender and intersex people – and for anyone who loves equality and freedom – in southern Africa. Its founding and its mission is rooted in the belief that the story of African struggles for gender justice is not just one of prejudice and casualty, but equally one of pride and power.

We are very proud of the work done by The Other Foundation's Samuel Shapiro on *Pride and Prejudice*.

– Neville Gabriel
Chief Executive Officer
The Other Foundation
www.theotherfoundation.org

Editor's note

THIS ANTHOLOGY WALKS THE LINE between all that is dissident and everything that is normative. The stories in this collection zigzag between a desire for justice and a refusal to be merely tolerated. In these pages you will find storylines that are achingly familiar, which play with tropes and mine them for truth. You will also find characters that come from the future, whose tenacity resists categorisation even as it reflects a resilience we have always demonstrated. This collection reflects a political moment across this continent, a moment that is defined by space and freedom even as these continue to be constrained. In other words, this is a queer collection.

    I edited this anthology, but we wrote this together. And I don't mean the authors and the photographers and poets and journalists and academics whose work you will find here. When I say we wrote this together, I mean we who are African: those of us who claim the identity that attaches to this continent in ways that are limitless rather than limiting. We wrote this. All of us wrote it. The homophobes and the resisters, the patriarchs and the subversives, the judges and the lawyers – we wrote this.

We began to write this book when we challenged the laws that made us criminals for daring to love. We scribbled ourselves into existence when we walked down the street like b-boys with caps turned backwards and did not cry when someone screamed 'lesbian' as though it were an epithet. The prologue of this book was written when we began to mourn en masse whenever women were killed, when we decided to be detectives, solving murders the police would not touch because there is little value attached to a woman's life.

The judges who selected the works that ended up in this anthology – and I am proud to have been one – read through hundreds of scores of stories. Much of what we read made us nod our heads and laugh and cry. We read many stories that were similar. Often we felt as though we were reading stories we already knew – and this was good because it reminded us that the book served a need. When the same story is told over and over again, it is because it has not been heard enough times, because the listeners are not listening.

In the end we chose these stories as emblems, as stand-ins for many others. We resisted the urge to embrace only what felt new and we resisted – equally – the impulse to reject that which made us uncomfortable because it was so new. We also resisted our impulse to publish only those stories that exploded myths. We chose a few that burrowed into old tropes in ways that were insightful or revelatory.

What you are holding in your hand then is not simply a collection of writing and imagery. This book is a shelter, a place where slums are not art, they are simply where we live. It's a place where albinos are not unicorns, they are only beautiful and ordinary. And it's a place where gays are pained and also completely conventional. In this book, strange choppers fly and Africa is a landscape not simply for the past but for projections of the future.

In its complexity and with its furious intellect, these stories say everything about how we have survived and why we continue to struggle to breathe. This book reflects the work of decades of activism against Aids and hetero-normativity, and the activism for dignity and feminism. It also reflects how far we have come in creating self-contained universes in which love and hilarity thrive even in the face of pain and suppression and violence.

This collection contains some of the best writing I have seen about the human condition. It is observant and witty and heart-breaking. It is as though each story and poem and image were fashioned from the hems of our mother's skirts and from the rage in our bellies. Taken together, the stories in this collection create their own language. They pay homage to the countries that suckled us – those places where mockery and shame rule but garner no respect from us. These stories are queer because they reflect our hybridity. They write our queerness into our love for DJ Banj and Anne Kansiime. They lean into our critical embrace of kasi style. These stories reject Western lenses that want to take our photos and evaporate our spirits; they take their own selfies and send them via WhatsApp to our fans.

This book is for anyone who has ever hungered for beauty. It is pockmarked and asymmetrical and so it is wondrous. Editing it has been a joy.

– Sisonke Msimang
Editor

JOINT WINNER

Poached eggs

FARAH AHAMED

'Marry me Nuru,' Jaffer said in his precise, measured tone, 'and together we'll build our future in this new independent republic.'

He was standing behind Nurbanu's typewriter and she was sitting at her desk at the chambers where she worked. She'd met him several months earlier when he'd come in to meet one of the lawyers and they'd struck up a friendship. Nuru had a Pitman's Secretarial Diploma and a driver's licence from the first Ladies Driving School in Nairobi. With her natural beauty and qualifications, she felt she deserved the care of a man who would cherish her. Jaffer was a successful self-made businessman. He was short, dark and stocky and less educated than Nuru, but she accepted his proposal because he was someone who appreciated her – why else would he speak about her and Kenyan politics in the same sentence?

The night they returned to Nairobi from their honeymoon in Mombasa, Nuru lay next to Jaffer in their new double bed. He in striped grey and white pyjamas and she in a floral nightie. She touched his shoulder; his back was to her. 'Jaffer?'

'Good night, Nuru,' he said. 'I'm meeting key officials in government tomorrow. I need my sleep.' He switched off the bedside lamp and pulled the bed clothes over his head.

Nuru thought of her new garden; the red hibiscus, pink bougainvillea and purple jacaranda were in full bloom. Tomorrow she'd lie under the jacaranda and look up at the sky through the leaves and branches. Unlimited possibilities lay ahead. She fell asleep listening to Jaffer's snores, dreaming she was driving a white Morris around Nairobi. Her arm was resting on the open window, and she was wearing fashionable dark glasses and an elegant scarf.

Jaffer employed Maria and Jacob to help Nuru with the household chores and garden. This left her with plenty of free time. After a month she said, 'I'd like to go back to working at Mr Seth's Chambers.'

'You can't do that, Nuru,' Jaffer said, standing in the middle of the doorway, his hand on the door knob. 'People will say I can't afford to take care of you.'

'But Mr Seth's ringing me today to confirm my start date.'

'Then tell him I said the wives of prosperous men don't work.' He looked at his watch. 'I'm late, Nuru. There are important people waiting to see me.'

She proffered her cheek, but he ran down the steps and drove off without a wave.

Nuru opened her wardrobe. She put on the clothes she used to wear to work: her court shoes, navy blue skirt and white blouse. She went from room to room feeling the different textures of the furniture: smooth, rough, coarse and grainy. Jaffer had arranged for the fixtures – beds, chairs, tables, stools, sofas and armchairs – to come before she'd moved in.

Every bedroom had its own colour scheme – pink and green, lime and yellow, blue and grey. She, too, was an object chosen by him. She fitted into the design and layout. Their bedroom window overlooked the garden with trim hedges, an even lawn and bushes pruned into geometric shapes. Jacob was sweeping the fallen flowers from under the jacaranda.

'Please let them be,' she called out. 'I like the purple carpet.'

'No, Mama,' Jacob said. 'Bwana Kubwa, our master, doesn't like anything out of its place.'

Jaffer arrived home early. Nuru was lying on the bed with a migraine. He took off his jacket and hung it on a chair. 'Today I accomplished everything I intended ahead of time,' he said, loosening his braces. 'It's all about proper management.' He pulled off the metal shirt-sleeve holders. 'What about you, Nuru, what did you do today?' he asked, removing his tie.

'The usual.'

'You have a headache, Nuru, because you're not organised.' He took a stack of papers from his briefcase. 'A list of things to do,' he said, pointing to the first page. 'Prepare Jaffer's breakfast. Supervise Maria and Jacob. Take siesta. Make dinner. Talk to Jaffer. Sleep.'

'I see,' Nuru said, turning the page.

'Ten carrots. Four onions. Ten tomatoes. Four loaves of sliced white bread. One chicken. Two pieces of tilapia fish. Six cartons of milk. Seven apples. Fourteen eggs.'

'What if we need other things?'

'You'll tell me and I'll prepare an additional list.'

'How can you be sure we'll need only fourteen eggs?'

'I'll have two every morning. But you won't be eating any, Nuru, because they give women health problems.'

'I didn't know that.'

'This is your budget for the week,' Jaffer said. 'Two hundred shillings for vegetables, two hundred for fruit, two hundred for the bakers, two hundred for the butchers, two hundred for groceries.'

'But these things don't all cost the same.'

'True, but you'll bargain in the market. Every shilling counts.'

She looked at the next page. 'A menu for breakfast, lunch and dinner?'

'Yes. For breakfast on Mondays I'll have an omelette, scrambled eggs on Tuesday, boiled on Wednesdays, poached on Thursdays and fried on Fridays. At the weekend I'll tell you the previous night for spontaneity.' He took the papers from her and smoothed out the creases. Then he showed her a red binder with a neat label: Nuru's Duties.

'These are important reference documents,' he said, arranging the contents inside. 'Keep them safe.' He put the file on the bureau. 'Ring my mother and get the recipes of my favourite foods. Follow exactly what she says and put her instructions in the file. And here's a calendar for you, too.'

'What's this for?' she said.

'On the days marked with a red cross you won't be sleeping here with me, you'll be in the pink and green room. I don't like it when you're unclean.' He unhooked his braces, put them on the dresser, and then sat down on the arm chair near the wardrobe. He pulled off his socks, rolled them in a ball and put them in the laundry basket. Then he took off his shirt, folded it neatly and placed it in the hamper. He removed his wallet from his trouser pocket and pulled out some notes. After counting, squaring and smoothing them down, he put them back. He undid his trousers, shook them out, doubled them and put them in the basket. 'Nuru,' he said, 'make sure Maria irons my clothes properly.'

He came and stood near the bed, wearing only his shorts and a white ribbed cotton vest, and smiled down at Nuru. He'd grown a belly in recent weeks and his shoulders were beginning to curve. He'd have a stoop and a big paunch, overhanging those skinny, hairless legs, when he was older.

'You're a lucky woman, Nuru.' He tucked his vest into his shorts and pulled them higher around his waist. 'I'm always one step ahead.'

'You've forgotten nothing,' she said, getting out of bed. They were the same height, and she looked him straight in the eye. He was greying at the temples and his hairline was receding.

'There's one more rule,' he said. 'A final, important, unwritten one. It's quite simple: I like the same thing no matter which day of the week.' He pushed her gently back onto the bed.

She imagined the mauve jacarandas falling on her; she'd heard it brought good luck.

Nuru turned the pages of the newspaper Jaffer had given her.

'You can read the *Daily Nation* once a week,' he said. 'But treat it with respect. I have to return it to the office.'

Nuru studied the paper. 'It says all voters should be registered. When can we do that?'

'I'll keep you informed,' he said. 'Please be gentler when you turn the pages, you're bending the edges.'

'There's excitement about the elections; I'd like to vote.'

'You don't need to worry about it, Nuru,' he said, taking the paper from her. 'We're one and the same, you and I.'

'You can't say that. We're different people.'

'Not anymore – you're part of me.'

'But it's one person, one vote.'

'Never mind what it says. You're my wife, we're one unit.' He folded the paper under his arm. 'And I've been thinking, from now on, no more English.'

'I don't understand,' she said. 'Do you mean in Kenya?'

'No, in this house. English is the language of our oppressors and we're an independent nation now.'

'What are we to speak then?'

'Gujrati, and only that.'

'But I think in English.'

'You can think in whatever language you like, Nuru. But you and I will speak in Gujrati. You'll just have to get used to it.'

'What purpose will that serve?'

'Speaking in our mother tongue will make our bond stronger,' he said. 'And whenever I get some spare time I'll teach you new Gujrati words. Our language is full of nuances. Take the word "you" for instance – it can be used respectfully or informally. So in future, always use the respectful version when addressing me.'

'Could you buy me a car?' Nuru asked one evening while they were eating dinner. She put her driver's licence on the table next to him. 'I paid for the lessons myself.'

'I'll take you wherever you need to go.' He mashed the rice, potatoes and curry on his plate with his fingers. 'Nothing beats my mother's cooking. You ought to learn from her.'

Nuru moved the rice around her plate with her fork. 'News Hour' was on the radio. After a round-up of the day's events, the newscaster reminded listeners that Kenya would soon be having its first election as an independent nation.

'KANU's going to win,' Jaffer said.

'You can't be so certain. Opposition parties like KADU also have support.'

'No, Mzee Jomo is not about to let any minority group challenge his party. We're a one-party state and Kenyatta has the ruling mandate. The elections are just a confirmation of his power.' He swiped the edge of his plate with his chubby forefinger and licked it. 'Like me, Kenyatta believes in centralised authority to keep people in line.'

Nuru went to the kitchen and scraped her dinner into the bin.

'Is that my mother's cooking you're wasting?' Jaffer said, coming to stand next to her.

'I've lost my appetite.'

'You're beginning to look thin, Nuru. People will say you're unhappy. Make an effort to eat a little extra at every meal, and if it's my mother's cooking, finish every grain.' He belched. 'Can you fetch me something for indigestion? I think I've overeaten.'

'My friend, Dr Stockley, was giving these away because he's returning to Britain,' Jaffer said, placing several thick volumes and booklets on the coffee table: *Radiant Health*, *Encyclopaedia of Diseases*, *Reader's Digest* and a book of Kenyan road maps. 'He remembered meeting you at our wedding and you saying you enjoyed reading.'

'Yes, I recall that conversation.'

'I told him married life keeps you busy and you don't have time to read now, but he insisted. There are more in the car.'

Nuru went through the books and arranged them in piles dividing them by subject. 'Don't waste your time, Nuru,' Jaffer said, 'just display them on the shelf according to height – that's how they look best. And don't leave them lying around the house.'

Aside from the ones relating to health and Kenyan geography, there was a Bible and several empty notebooks. Nuru decided to use one as a journal. In the afternoons she'd spend a few hours writing and then she would lie under the muslin net draped over the bed and watch the whirring ceiling fan. Sometimes a mosquito landed on the mesh and scratched at the fabric trying to get in. She would watch it until it flew off and feel suffocated.

Nuru watched Jaffer spoon the egg into his mouth and wipe the dribble from his lips. 'This is a few seconds too soft, Nuru.' The newscaster on the radio was talking about the elections. Jaffer turned it off. 'You aren't listening to me.'

'Sorry, what did you say?'

'My eggs should be boiled for three minutes and fifteen seconds.'

'Who was at the Freemasons meeting last night?'

'I've taken an oath, so I can't tell you. They're men of my calibre and tastes.'

'What are they saying about the elections?'

'Nothing you'd understand, Nuru.'

'I was up half the night waiting for you. Where were you?'

'There are important new opportunities I'm exploring.'

'What are they?'

'For God's sake, Nuru, I wish you wouldn't bother me with your questions. I know what I'm doing and it's high time you did too. Make sure my eggs are done exactly right tomorrow.'

Nuru found the newspaper Jaffer had forgotten to take to work lying on the kitchen counter. She turned to the letters section and copied down the postal address at the bottom of the page.

Daily Nation, Nairobi
27 March 1963

Dear Editor,

On the eve of Kenya's first elections as an independent state, when women have an equal right to vote for the first time, it is important that women in the new republic know their limits in Kenyan society. I wonder if the *Daily Nation* would be interested in publishing a guide on how they should behave.

If you think this is something that would appeal to your readership, I could send you one rule a week, including recipes and home remedies for common ailments, such as indigestion, which afflict men. I am enclosing a sample for your consideration.

I look forward to hearing from you.

Yours faithfully,
Mrs Nurbanu Muljiani Encl.

Women, Know Your Place
1. If your husband tells a witty story, be sure to laugh – his jokes are always funny. Be fragile and sweet; these qualities will make you delightful and desirable.
2. Never question your husband; he knows best. Be quick to admit you know less than him. Be plain and simple with your thoughts; let your natural sweetness shine through.

3. Before your husband arrives home in the evening, make a hot or cool drink, arrange a comfortable pillow in his armchair and wipe the tables. Change your dress, apply lipstick and dab on perfume. Soothe him with your delicate demeanour.
4. Allow your husband to talk first – what he has to say is much more important than anything you can offer. Listen attentively and reassure him with a pleasing voice.
5. Never discuss politics with your husband; your foolish and dangerous thoughts will embarrass him and arouse his contempt. Appearing over-educated and expressing opinions will lead to stress and premature ageing.
6. Mix one teaspoonful of Eno's Fruit Salts in half a glass of water if your husband has acidity or heartburn. His overindulgence is a measure of your prowess as a cook.

When she'd finished writing, she put the letter and article in an envelope and asked Maria to take it to the post office.

The next morning Nuru was in the kitchen preparing Jaffer's breakfast. The window looked out onto the garden; she had a sudden longing to see unpruned bougainvillaea bushes in deep orange and red, and sprawling morning glory creepers in white and purple. She took the tray of eggs from the fridge, stood staring at it, then picked up an egg and rolled it from one palm to the other, feeling its smooth, curved surface. She broke it into a cup, then did the same with a second egg, and, with a fork, whisked the yellow and white.

Slowly, she raised the frothy mixture, tipped it into her mouth and swallowed. She wiped her lips with a tissue, went into the dining room and poured herself some tea.

'Where are my poached eggs?' Jaffer said, sitting down at the head of the table. 'It's Thursday.' He tucked a starched napkin under his chin.

'They slipped from my hands.'

He banged his fist on the table. 'Don't let it happen again.'

'I'll try not to,' she said. 'If you like I can use tomorrow's eggs and prepare them for you right away.'

'You'll do no such thing,' he said, flinging off his napkin. 'There are two eggs for each day, so leave it at that. Next time, treat them with care; they're very fragile.'

'I'd like to meet my friends sometime,' Nuru said at breakfast a few days later. 'Friends?' Jaffer asked. He applied a thick layer of butter to his toast.

'Yes, and my family. You're always meeting yours.'

'You don't need them, Nuru, they'll only gossip about us. My friends are different – they discuss important issues.'

'Such as?'

'The future of our country.'

'I've been thinking about that too.'

'Kenya needs active citizens and I think the time is right for us to make our contribution.'

'I couldn't agree more,' she said. 'Today's the day we'll vote.'

'Don't be stupid, Nuru, I'm talking about having children.' He left the room and came back with the calendar. 'I'll do my duty on the days marked with black stars. At the end of the month we'll tally the score and record the number in the corner. That way we'll monitor our progress.' He sat down, putting the calendar next to her plate. 'Now, Nuru, where are my eggs?'

'What about voting?'

'You know how to ruin a man's mood in the morning, don't you, Nuru? If you have nothing of interest to say, don't say it.' He left the dining room, slamming the door behind him. She watched from the window as he drove off in his blue Anglia.

Maria came in to clear the table. 'Where's the nearest polling station, Maria?'

'At the primary school in the market, Mama.'

Nuru walked with Maria to the market through the gullies of kiosks selling fruits and vegetables. A stray dog blocked their path and Maria shooed it away. A goat stood grazing on a clump of dry grass and chickens scuttled around.

'KANU special,' a vendor called out, holding up a bunch of blemished bananas. 'Not today,' Nuru said.

They stopped to watch an old woman with a khanga tied around her head, sitting on a low stool in front of a stove. She spooned boiled maize and beans from the pot onto a tin plate and served it to a man standing there.

'Our great nation has space for only one party,' he said in Kiswahili, taking the food from her, 'and one man.'

'You're wrong,' the woman said. 'We need women in government, like Makumbi in Uganda and Lameck in Tanzania.'

'Those are just rumours by *wakorofi*, troublemakers.'

'I heard it on the radio.'

'Don't believe everything you hear; women should stick to gardening, cooking and bearing children. *Shamba, chakula na watoto.* Leave the business of running the country to us men.'

'It's only a matter of time. One day the women of Maendeleo ya Wanawake will have power.' The woman placed her things in her sisal basket, and swung it over her back. 'A flag blows in the direction of the wind,' she said. 'And the winds of change have begun.'

The following day, Nuru was in the dining room pouring Jaffer's tea. He came in and stood behind his chair. 'Jam, butter, toast and tea,' he said, enunciating each word. 'But no eggs. What's going on, Nuru?'

'They were overcooked. I've thrown them in the bin.' Jaffer thumped the back of the chair.

'Maria,' he shouted. She appeared at the door. 'You're paid to help my wife in the kitchen. Can you explain this?'

'*Mimi sijui, Mzee,*' Maria said. 'Me, I don't know.'

'I'm surrounded by ignorant and incompetent women.'

'Mistakes happen sometimes,' Nuru said.

'Not in my house they don't.' He walked out of the room banging the door. A few minutes later, he was back. 'Nuru, Jacob's just told me you went to the market yesterday. Why did you go? It wasn't market day according to my schedule.'

'To vote.'

'Nuru,' he shouted. 'Stop your meddling. Our country's politics is a delicate business. Don't interfere, do you understand?'

That night after Jaffer got into bed, Nuru went around tucking the mosquito net under the mattress.

'I don't like being defied, Nuru,' he said from behind the mesh. 'It doesn't bode well for our future.' He placed the *Daily Nation* on her pillow. 'Even Kenyatta faces no opposition now because KADU has dissolved itself and merged with KANU.'

Nuru lifted the net on her side and settled down next to him. She turned the pages of the paper and stopped at the advertisement for a Morris. 'That's the car I want – the two-door model.'

'Let me see that,' he said. 'More Mini magic, what nonsense. You can't even handle eggs without an accident, never mind a steering wheel.'

Nuru sat on the sofa reading one of Dr Stockley's books. She looked up when Jaffer came in. 'You're home early.'

'You're the talk of the town, Nuru.' Jaffer flung the newspaper down next to her. She picked it up.

'Picture my humiliation,' he said, 'when John mentioned his wife had been praising your column in the *Daily Nation*.'

'I wanted it to be a surprise.'

'It was a bombshell. I had no idea what he was talking about.'

'What did he say?'

'He congratulated me for being the perfect husband. I didn't know what to say, so I told him I always did my best.' He paused. 'When I got back to the office I read your piece but I'll tell you what really annoyed me.'

'Yes?'

'The title should be: "Know Your Place According to Jaffer".'

'I'll have a word with the editor tomorrow,' she said. 'By the way, there'll be no eggs for the rest of the week.'

'Nuru, are my ears deceiving me?'

'I was preparing the dinner,' she said. 'A recipe from your mother. I had to remove the eggs from the fridge to reach something behind them. And I'm afraid I dropped the entire tray.'

A place of greater safety
Homosexuality, homelessness and HIV in Cape Town

BEYERS DE VOS

NOWHERE ELSE TO GO

IT IS A SUNNY AUTUMN MORNING in April when Peter wakes up to the sounds of his boyfriend making breakfast.

Peter watches as Frans dishes up the food, hating him for the mess he is making. 'Don't you want to put the lid back?' Peter asks scornfully. Frans turns around slowly; the soft redness of a tik high swims in his eyes.

Peter's relationship with Frans has been floundering on and off for over five years – this latest instalment is barely eight months old. The affair is passionate and drug-fuelled. A deeply flawed symbiosis: Frans is a well-known gangster and in Manenberg – a poverty-rich Cape Town suburb where Peter's homosexuality could mean death – Frans provides necessary security. In return, Peter provides Frans with sex.

'What did you say to me?'

Things have been tense between them lately. Frans is possessive and paranoid. He doesn't allow Peter to go out by himself and he refuses to let him leave the borders of Manenberg. He flies into fits of rage and gets jealous if Peter speaks to other men, even if they are 'straight' or 'married'. Frans understands that these labels mean nothing. Frans is also a habitual rapist, often overpowering Peter, holding a knife to his throat and forcing sex on him. Peter stopped thinking of it as rape after the third time.

When Peter isn't high, he is scared. But he is high most of the time.

Peter ducks as a dirty plate crashes behind him. A shard of porcelain strikes the back of his head. Before he knows what's happening, Frans is on top of him, fists pounding into him. Peter knows this routine well: he folds his thin body into the foetal position and waits for Frans's rage to subside.

Frans runs out of energy and his fists slow down and then eventually they stop altogether.

Frans stands and walks over to the doorway; he stands there as though he is guarding it.

Peter gets up and, like he has done so many times before, begins to pack his bags. His lip is bleeding; his arms, which have taken the brunt of the beating, are stinging fiercely.

'I'm going to kill you,' Frans says.

Peter considers the many threats Frans has made before. He thinks about the cycle of beatings and what his life has become. He expects Frans to stop him when he walks out the door, but the stronger man stands aside and lets him go. It's a small conciliatory gesture, and its gentleness almost makes Peter change his mind. But he doesn't.

No. I have to leave this time; I have to make a change.

He has been thinking about it for months. It is now or never. The words of Devon and Denise and the judge who gave him a second chance – and many people besides – mark out his steps for him. He walks away.

He doesn't know where he is going.

ON THE ROAD

The walk from Manenberg to Heideveld Station takes Peter roughly 30 minutes. He walks down Duinefontein Road, passing squat, wind-worn houses. Some are brightly painted in blues and pinks and yellows. Others are nothing more than shacks. Someone decided to plant palm trees next to the road in a patch of tall grass – the only patch of grass in a world of grey dust – perhaps to make this stretch of road more attractive or more exotic. It didn't work. Litter gets whipped around in the breeze; the poorer cousin of tumbleweed.

At Heideveld Station Peter waits 15 minutes for the train to Cape Town city centre. It costs R7. It takes another 33 minutes to reach Cape Town, the train idling its way from the Cape Flats – hidden, unseen – to the very heart of historic Cape Town, proud and beautiful between mountain and harbour.

It is busy at Cape Town Station – too busy to exit immediately. It takes Peter half an hour to get out of the building.

The sky is darkening, night is coming, but he knows where he is going now. He has only one option.

To get to his destination will take roughly 40 minutes. He will need to walk; he doesn't have money for the bus or a taxi.

He walks up, up, upward, via Adderley Street and then Long Street. Past the Company Gardens and over De Vaal Road, into the border of Oranjezicht.

The Gardens Centre stretches into the sky on his left – ugly but familiar.

He carries only one bag. It contains:

One wallet (R20)
One ID book
One yellow T-shirt (stained)
One pair of old black sneakers (ripped)
One Bible (new)

He wanders through the still leafy streets of Oranjezicht, climbing upward all the time. Along the way he stops at a church. He sits quietly in the back, listening to the service. He prays.

He walks on.

Finally, as he crests the hill, with the inner city lit up below him and the mountain towering above, he sees it: the yellow house.

He waits at the front gate, staring at the broad street and the beautiful houses.

When the caretaker arrives, he lets Peter in. He gives him a cup of coffee and a sandwich. He takes him to the laundry room and Peter selects a few items of clothing. He shows Peter to a bed.

There are other people in the house. They are wary. They have their own problems.

Peter falls asleep knowing he is safe.

THE YELLOW HOUSE

Wednesdays are trash days in Oranjezicht.

All over the neighbourhood small gangs of trash-divers are searching through the large black bins outside every house in the hope of finding something – anything – to eat or sell.

The bin in front of the yellow house has just been emptied into the bowels of a large, noisy truck, but the young woman sitting on the curb has managed to salvage something. On her lap she has a large box of kiwi fruit that is still edible. She cleans each fruit carefully with the hem of her white dress, scrubbing away the layer of filth that has contaminated the fruit. She is meticulous, intent. She does not hear the calls of her companions who are dawdling further down the street. Two children sit obediently by her side; they will have something to eat today.

But she isn't why I am here. My business is with the house.

I had heard about Pride Shelter from a friend, and was immediately intrigued by all the stories that seemed to have lived in that house. I wanted to reach out to them. I wanted to know them.

The house is tall and crooked. It stands with its back to the mountain, facing the City Bowl, which is swirling with dark clouds this morning. It is a wet day yet this little corner of the city, the little pocket snuggled high against the breast of Table Mountain, has somehow managed to escape the weather for the moment. It is lit up with golden sunlight. The air is sweet. It reeks with the earthy scent of seed pods – brown and damp – that have been discarded in their thousands by the trees lining the street.

The house is modest but stately. It is one of the first houses built in Oranjezicht and it stands on one of the original plots cut out of the Oranjezicht farm in 1900, when that fertile land was abandoned to make way for the development of a new neighbourhood. There is something about the house that can make you forget you are in the twenty-first century; it envelops you in its history.

I walk through the gate, closing it on the back of the young woman sitting in the street cleaning her fruit.

I have stepped into another world.

This is Pride Shelter, a homeless shelter for members of the LGBTI (Lesbian, Gay, Bisexual, Transgender and Intersex) community. As I approach the front door, two men appear on the stoep like sentinels, flanking the door with guarded curiosity.

'Is Matron here?' I ask tentatively.

Matron's real name is Janette Richter but no one calls her that. She is simply Matron. She is standing in the doorway. She has large, expressive eyes and spiky, red-tinged hair. Her smile widens when she introduces herself and welcomes me into the house. The two men disappear.

She asks me if I would like a tour. I would love one.

The entrance hall is akin to a hotel lobby – sparse, official and filled with brochures. The room is dominated by a broad staircase, beautifully carved from dark, shiny wood. Directly to the left of the front door is a room that Matron reckons used to be a ballroom, but is perhaps too small to have ever hosted a ball. It was probably a formal dining room. The room now contains a rough circle of a dozen office chairs and some bookshelves. 'We sometimes rent this out to people for gatherings,' Matron says, which isn't strictly speaking true. It is set aside for AA meetings, in support of residents with addiction problems, but Matron doesn't trust me enough to say so. Not yet.

A narrow hallway leads off from the entrance hall into the bowels of the house: Matron's office, the kitchen and the laundry room, where two dogs are sleeping. The kitchen is a large, open space, cool and blue in the early morning. The house rules are pasted on the fridge door: chore wheels, curfews, a list of punishable transgressions and various timetables keeping track of who is at work and when. Residents of Pride Shelter need to either have a job or be out looking for one. They are discouraged from idling the day away inside the house.

The bedrooms are on the top floor. Most of them have been converted into dormitories. I stand on one of the large airy balconies and drink in the city. Matron points out the back garden, currently under construction and therefore off limits. This garden rises in tiers towards the back fence, through which the Malteno Reservoir – where electricity in Cape Town was generated for the very first time – is sparkling in the sun.

The house is rented from the City of Cape Town for R650 a month and is completely reliant on the kindness of strangers. Most of the residents are people who have suffered abuse or persecution based on their sexual orientation or gender identity and have been left homeless. Pride Shelter is not meant to be a permanent solution – people can live here until they get back on their feet, but then they need to move on. Pride Shelter was opened in 2010. The project was initiated by the Triangle Project, an LGBTI charity that provides counselling services to gay and transwomen and men in Cape Town. Many of those accessing mental health services from the Triangle Project had been left destitute and needed housing. When it opened its doors, the first two residents (a married gay couple from Port Elizabeth, chased away by angry parents) were already sitting on the front porch. All the furniture in the house, every bunk bed and every chair, was donated by the surrounding community.

Today, five years later, the project is beginning to break even and donations continue flooding in.

Despite these frugalities, this house – with its high, embossed ceilings and fireplaces that would not be out of place in a Bishopscourt mansion, its timeworn wooden floors, ivy-covered walls and wrap-around balconies – has a former glory that has been somehow intangibly preserved in its own atmosphere. Its scents and spaces evoke an unspecific splendour of early twentieth-century Cape Town. History is all around.

We end our tour on the far side of the house, staring through large, faded windows. Matron points to the mountain, which can be seen from almost every room in the house. I will soon come to discover how important the presence of the mountain – beaming blue and beautiful, like a guardian angel – is to residents of Pride Shelter.

Residents like Peter.

JUST PETER

I meet Peter not long after his arrival at Pride Shelter. He is not the reason I came to Pride Shelter. I came seeking a story about refugees fleeing sexual persecution. Before Peter, I did meet a refugee from Uganda, who spoke of how the shelter was helping him restore his faith in humanity, but he only consented to speak to me briefly, before hastily retreating from my pen. I also spoke to a young woman who had been contemplating suicide; she said the house saved her life. There was also an elderly man who suffered a stroke and was abused by his caretaker and had nowhere else to turn.

Each of them was wary, holding something back. I could see that trust was hard to come by, a currency they clearly no longer traded in.

But Peter is different. He smiles when he introduces himself. 'Peter,' he says. Peter is short and slight, in his early thirties, with cropped hair and animated brown eyes, one of which still has the purple shadow of a bruise burning beneath it.

'Peter who?' I ask.

'Just Peter.'

He is open and willing to talk, yes, but he won't surrender his surname. And he has fighting words when we first sit down to the interview. 'We don't all want to talk about our situations. I don't know who you are or where you come from. People who come here are fragile, you know?' He pauses. 'Where do we start?'

He gives me a rapid-fire history of his life so far, and his story instantly grips me.

- He knew he was gay from a very young age. The house he grew up in was conservative. Religion mattered and there was no question of being gay; no room to question your sexuality.
- By the time he was twenty he was spending his days lounging around his parents' house. He liked drinking and smoking weed. He was trying to grapple with an increasingly insistent desire to explore his suppressed attraction to men.
- He became a father. Her name is Robin, and she is an obvious source of pride.

I ask him if I can meet Robin, but he shakes his head. She doesn't know about any of this: his HIV or his being gay or his homelessness. Under what pretence would I see her? 'And her mother wouldn't allow it.'

'And,' I ask, 'you're not married to her mother?'

He shakes his head and explains. On the day that Andile, Robin's mother, found out she was pregnant, her family marched across the Cape Flats – the nearly ten kilometres from Gugulethu to Elsie's River – to come and negotiate lobola. Peter's father took him into the bedroom before they arrived. 'You're still young,' he told his son. 'Andile is still at school. I married your mother because your grandfather demanded it, because it was his culture. It was the way it was done. But you don't have to do this. I won't force you. It is your decision whether you want to marry this girl or not.'

Peter decided he would not sacrifice himself at the altar of expectation.

Robin was born while Andile was finishing matric. For the first few years of her life, she lived in Peter's parents' house being raised by her grandmother. But Peter barely saw her. He was out discovering new attractions: drugs and boys. His decision not to marry the mother of his child confirmed something to his community – it emasculated him. It was after this that strangers began to call him 'moffie' on the streets. 'It is expected, you know, in so-called coloured communities to have a child and get married and be straight and look after your family.'

Whenever someone asked him directly about his sexuality he would deflect the question. 'What are they going to do with the information?' he asks. 'It won't change the course of history. Sometimes people want to know just to know. It won't contribute to my life to tell them anything.'

Peter brought his first boy home when his daughter was still a baby, living with him and his parents in their house.

COMING OUT

When Peter brings the man home, his parents are watching the news. They watch it at seven o'clock every night, and have done so ever since Peter can remember. A story about the national elections is on. Thabo Mbeki's ANC will form the third national government within the month. Peter's father doesn't like Thabo Mbeki.

It is a small flat: one bedroom, a bathroom and a kitchen-cum-living room that is bathed in the artificial white glare emanating from the TV. Lights are used sparingly in this house; electricity is expensive. The smell of curry, a family favourite, scents the night. But dinner is already over.

Peter is rarely home anymore and his mother has stopped preparing meals for him. When he walks through the door, they look up silently. Peter stares back defiantly. His parents are both gaunt. His mother is emaciated: she has been plump all her life but has recently lost a lot of weight. His father is very tall and very thin, with deep-set eyes and no hair. They are proud people, but they say nothing. Robin is asleep on the couch between them. She is nearly six years old. Peter has spent the money set aside for her birthday present on tik and on the sex he will be having tonight, but no one knows that yet. Peter is hanging on the shoulders of Miss M, a notorious local drag queen and self-identified moffie. They are both high. Miss M is in her full gear: a pink miniskirt, which has become her signature, and stiletto heels. Peter says nothing to his mute parents. His mother breaks out into one of her regular coughing fits. A lifelong smoker, she has developed serious emphysema. Peter ignores it. He takes Miss M into the bedroom and closes the door behind them.

Tonight they will have loud sex in his parents' bed; his parents will sleep on the couch.

The next morning when he wakes up, Miss M isn't next to him. He can hear hushed voices coming from the next room. He senses danger. He has pushed his humble, reserved father too far. He dresses quickly and slowly makes his way to the kitchen, afraid of what he will find. He knows that there are people besides his parents in the house; he knows too that Miss M has been hauled away and beaten by angry parents before.

When he walks into the kitchen, it is like sun breaking through the cloud. Miss M is standing with his hand around Peter's mother. They are in a fit of giggles, huddled over the stove, cooking breakfast. His father is sitting at the kitchen table. 'Morning,' his father says, 'would you like some coffee?'

That is how Peter comes out to his parents, although he never speaks to them about it again.

Nowadays, he no longer has the time or energy to worry about what people think or the mistakes he has made. He has developed a stoic, philosophical response to the question of telling his family about his life. 'It makes me sad that I am not able to share what I am going through with them. But at the same time, I've made peace with that. I have other people I can share with. Strangers, like you.'

A GAY OL' TIME

Moffie. Fag. Queer. They all mean the same thing. Each has been a slur and an embrace, possessed and dispossessed by different communities at different times for different reasons. Each has slid down the dark linguistic spiral from pejorative to word of empowerment to pejorative and back up again.

'Moffie' made its debut in the language of District Six, the inner-city suburb of early apartheid Cape Town where a large and vibrant coloured community flourished before their forced removals to the Cape Flats. It was a non-pejorative used to describe drag queens, flamboyant gay men who dressed as women and were a common feature of the Mardi Gras-style carnivals that were a part of the culture of that community. It was a word that travelled – it went with the coloured community to their new homes. It survives today in the vernacular of those communities and others, and it has undergone various changes. Most recently it has been usurped by the conservative Afrikaans-speaking white community, and is being used as a derogatory term as hate speech. But on the Cape Flats it survives as part term of endearment (if you're a drag queen) and part insult (if you are not).

Cross-dressing in District Six was an acceptable way for gay men to make themselves visible, to become part of the community. At the same time, cross-dressing forced many gay men to give up their masculinity. There was no such thing as both. If they kept within the feminine gender role they had been assigned, they were more easily accepted in the wider community. Sex with a moffie was acceptable if you were a heterosexual man if it was discreet and kept hidden – and if it was only sex. No relationships. No love. But men who self-identified as gay and refused to also give up their gender roles did not fit into an easy space. The repercussions of being gay and refusing to be a moffie were often swift and severe.

In the modern coloured community, there is a new negotiation underway. The negotiation between seeking limited socially acceptable homosexuality by becoming a moffie, which Peter regards as an act of disempowerment, or trying to be a gay man who refuses to succumb to the role set aside for him by society. And, of course, within communities dominated by both Christian and Muslim doctrine, neither course is necessarily safe.

'Growing up on the Cape Flats is not easy. Because you have to have this façade or persona: all manly and no one is going to touch me. Men are not allowed to cry. Everything is hardcore. And that is why a lot of men turn to substance abuse, because they just want to escape. During the day, they are these butch, hardcore, you-don't-mess-with-me type guys and in the evening, when everything is much calmer and they have indulged in whichever substance is their preference, they seek out people of the same sex. And even though they have wives and girlfriends, they won't go home. They seek shelter with gays. That's not healthy, that's not healthy.'

Sexuality on the Cape Flats is saturated with suspicion. You do not know who you can trust with your thoughts – especially if those thoughts stray anywhere beyond conservative conventions. Sex is between a married man and woman. Anything else isn't spoken about out. Peter knows, because so many married men living straight lives have sought out his company under the cover of darkness. He also knows that there are neighbours and friends who pretend to be homophobic to fit in, to protect themselves. He believes that there is, and has always been, a lot of homophobia on the Cape Flats. In his experience, many heterosexual people secretly experiment with same-sex sexual encounters on the Flats. 'You can access it fairly easily,' Peter says.

He thinks this secrecy is a big part of the problem: it stigmatises homosexuality and it turns it into a never-ending well of confusion and shame, and anyone who is brave enough to be openly gay is resented. You are either homophobic or homosexual; you are either a man or you are gay, and if you choose the latter you forfeit your rights as a man. In-between is not something that exists in these spaces; boundaries are pre-set and immovable. There is no room for shades of grey.

Except, maybe, if you are a moffie.

Peter distributes gay people on the Cape Flats into two categories: people who have no choice but to come out because of how effeminate (fem) they are and those who are still in hiding.

'So, ja, there are people on the Cape Flats who are openly gay. But it's a daily battle. You have to constantly fend off people. But even being a man is a daily struggle. If people are hungry, you can't really tell them about the church or God or homophobia. I want to know what I am going to eat tonight, so I don't have time for your yap-yap or your self-righteousness,' he says, the light tones of mimicry heightening his voice.

As a result, Peter gets attention if he walks down the streets by himself. Jeers, catcalls, threats. 'It hardens you,' he says. 'It prepares you, but I don't know what for. You get used to it, anyway. It's sad growing up knowing you won't be allowed to be ...' he pauses, '... who you want to be.'

But he has a surprising compassion for those men who persecute him for his sexuality. 'I think they [straight men] are struggling the most. They are the ones who have issues, because they are brought up to have a specific purpose: you look after your family, you don't cry and you need to be hard and you don't talk about your feelings. Keeping stuff to yourself can't be easy. It's detrimental, you know?

'At least gay people can, in some way, express themselves. If you hide who you are it's destructive. And that's why people go out of their communities, secretively, to do their own thing. To go to escort agencies, where no one knows them.'

Is that what he did?

Yes, he nods. That is exactly what he did: he fled the Flats to carve out a new identity for himself in Cape Town, ran away from his family and his responsibilities and the warped ideology of manhood. He lost himself in drugs and sex and rock 'n roll.

He tells me a story.

THE AFTER-9 BOYS

One night, not long after his daughter is born, a friend asks Peter to accompany him into the city centre. He says he wants to show him something. A surprise.

Isaac and Peter have known each other for a few months. They sleep together casually. Mainly they do drugs together.

They leave Manenberg at dusk, and before they have reached the end of the road, they light up a joint; tonight is going to be a party. The drive from the Cape Flats into the heart of Cape Town is just long enough for them to achieve a good high.

They park a few streets up from the Company Gardens. They are in a quiet residential street, standing in front of a modest house painted white. It looks like every other house in the street, innocuous and dull. But Peter is captivated by the relative affluence of the area – he does not know anyone so distant from his life on the Cape Flats. Before this, he had only been into the city centre a handful of times.

Isaac knocks. A woman answers the door. She is older and beautiful. She grew up on the Cape Flats, too, but she now resides in this house. She invites them in. Her name is Maureen and she is the madam of this brothel, where men have sex with men discreetly. She and Isaac are good friends; Isaac supplies the drugs Maureen keeps in-house for clients.

That night Peter, Maureen and Isaac get high together. It is the first time he uses cocaine. Peter becomes enchanted with Maureen and the two of them become fast friends. She introduces him to all her boys who are on duty throughout the night. She even gives him a free ride. On the house.

After that, he and Isaac make the trip to her house once a week. For the first time Peter can engage in gay sex freely and away from the prying eyes of his community. He loves it.

Soon enough, he is asked to audition for Maureen.

He is ushered into a room full of shadows. The curtains are drawn and the lights switched off. A woman he does not know is sitting in a single chair; there is no other furniture. Maureen is not there. He is asked to recite his biography: age, sexual history, medical condition. These facts are accepted at face value. His persona is assessed: who will he be for the clients, which personality will he be selling?

Then he is asked to undress. He is asked to pleasure himself.

The woman he is performing for will decide whether he is someone clients will find attractive.

Does he fit into a body type and look that is not currently available on the menu?

He does. Slim. Small. Well built.

Brown.

Will he be the surfer dude or the fem guy or the muscular dude?

He'll be the listener – getting clients to confide in him, trust him, be intimate with him. For those clients that want more than a fuck.

Will he be dominant or submissive?

Submissive, but with bite.

'Okay. You start tonight.'

A typical night as a rent boy involves sitting in a room behind a one-way mirror in only your underwear. If a client comes in, the parlour's sex workers introduce themselves one by one and the client takes his (or her) pick. Peter entertains two to three clients a night, for R1 000 an hour. Unprotected sex is extra. Fetish sex is extra. Drugs are extra.

He is shocked to discover most of his clients are married professionals, lawyers or doctors, or come from deeply religious institutions. His client list reads like a list of clichés: a lawyer who just wants to talk to someone, a businessman who flies him up to Johannesburg for a weekend, a doctor who has a thing for leather. He has a regular customer who is a priest from a nearby parish. He calls them the after-9 boys: those men who identify as straight but who come seeking same-sex companionship 'after nine, ten or eleven at night because they are high and don't want to go back to their wives'.

It is one of these men, he thinks, who eventually gives him HIV.

Not Frans?

No, he says, not someone who loves him.

I ask him, while we sit in the sunny bay window of the ballroom now used for AA meetings, why, if these brothels are so well known, so easy to access, so open, they never get shut down or raided by the police. How are these places so permissible?

He shrugs. 'Sometimes the police are our clients. Otherwise, that's just the way it is.' His time at Maureen's doesn't last long. His stints never do.

He does it for two months or three or four, before he moves back to Elsie's River and his parents' house.

But he keeps coming back to it, to support his ever-expanding drug habit. It is his fifth or sixth spell as a rent boy, working for a much more famous brothel called The Barracks, when his mother dies. It's 2004, the same year that Robin moved in with Andile. The death of his mother sends him over a ledge he had refused to fall off before: he begins using tik. To maintain this addiction, he starts working extra shifts. He moves to Cape Town permanently and begins trolling the local gay-bar scene looking for clients.

This time he stays for years. He begins selling his wares on the street.

When his father dies in 2012, he missed the funeral because no one knew where he was.

Working for an agency comes with a certain amount of security. But working the streets enveloped him in a new kind of darkness. There is no one to make sure you get paid, there is no one to make sure you aren't beaten up. It takes several years to use up all the favours he can call in, to outstay all his welcomes, but eventually he runs out of places to live, out of work and out of hope.

He is only now, years later, starting to forgive himself for that life. 'If God can forgive me 70 times a day, then who am I not to forgive myself?' he asks. 'I ruined my flesh, but I haven't ruined my spirit.'

Will he ever go back to it?

No, he won't. Even if by the end of this week he doesn't know where his next meal is going to come from, he won't ever return to that life.

He is adamant, he is sure.

A MEDITATION ON HOMELESSNESS

Homelessness is a difficult thing to navigate in South Africa. In a country so ravaged by poverty, where unemployment is endemic and the promise by national government to provide housing is still being rolled out, there exists a schism within the very definition of 'homeless'.

There are those who are chronically homeless, people who have been born into homelessness. And there is sudden homelessness: brought on by a crisis, by unemployment or violence. Andrew Massyn, one of the directors of the Pride Shelter board of trustees, who I meet in his office in Rondebosch one afternoon to get background on the project – and permission to visit the actual house – puts it this way: 'Homelessness in South Africa has become a way of life. Those are depressing circumstances, but it isn't a crisis. Sudden homelessness is a crisis.'

He stops there and looks at me knowingly; his inference is clear. Pride Shelter caters to the latter. It is not a night shelter; it is not a permanent solution. Pride Shelter is certainly one of a kind in South Africa, and I find no evidence of anything else like it in the rest of Africa either, although there are plenty of reasons not to advertise places like Pride Shelter on a continent so hostile to homosexuality.

Because the unemployment rate is so high, because informal housing is such a significant part of the way many South Africans live, tracking down a statistic quantifying the number of homeless people in this country is near impossible. And there is no research being done into what percentage of homeless people in South Africa is LGBTI and what kind of discrimination, if any, there exists against them. American research estimates between 20 and 30 per cent of homeless Americans are gay or lesbian, but this is not a transplantable statistic.

Besides, it is a difficult thing to measure, because homeless people would not necessarily identify as LGBTI even if they were asked. And unlike in the Western world, people in South Africa would be far less likely to be homeless because they are homosexual; their sexuality is just another on a list of factors contributing to their situation.

Nevertheless, Pride Shelter is clearly necessary. The residents and owners agree on one thing: it has saved many lives. LGBTI people in South Africa, many of whom were not used to or uncomfortable in overnight shelters, needed a place free of discrimination and abuse that could provide them with the shelter they needed. Very much ahead of the global trend to make homeless shelters more accessible to LGBTI citizens that is currently sweeping across America and Canada, Pride Shelter opened its doors.

Peter has experienced discrimination in other shelters he has frequented and he says he stays away from state hospitals on the Cape Flats because the health practitioners there won't keep your sexuality, or your HIV status, confidential. The news infiltrates the community because everyone knows everyone. 'You feel violated. Actually, it hurts.'

Peter has put his finger on the stigma surrounding homosexuality and HIV in communities all over South Africa. This is why he prefers the anonymity of organisations like Health4Men and the safety of a space like Pride Shelter – places where he can be just Peter. Not a moffie or a boyfriend or a father or someone who is HIV positive. Just Peter.

IN THE VALLEY OF THE SHADOW OF DEATH

While he is living on the street and addicted to tik, Peter seeks out Health4Men. It is a men's health clinic offering free medical care. They diagnose him with HIV.

It is Health4Men that first referred him to Pride Shelter. But he doesn't go. He thinks he has no future, and so there is no point in a safe house. 'I thought I would use and use and use and use and if I die, I die.'

HIV infection rates among the men who have sex with men (MSM) population group in South Africa, and worldwide, is consistently higher than other population groups. Approximately 5 per cent of South African men are homosexual, or are men who have sex with men, to use the term preferred by researchers, and an estimated 30 to 50 per cent of these men are HIV positive.

For a second, Peter becomes a statistic in front of my eyes. He is textbook. It is clear from Peter's background that his social and cultural environments limited his ability to identify as gay. In the coloured community of the Cape Flats, there is a definite correlation between the level of poverty and the prevalence of stigma. Manenberg, where Peter has lived on and off since 2004, for example, has higher levels of homophobia than other, more affluent coloured areas.

Peter's life exemplifies all the structural inequalities that make life difficult for men who have sex with men. Study after study tells us men like Peter are at a higher risk of contracting HIV than other population groups because the cards are stacked against them. And this stigma around homosexuality has a measurable effect on HIV-linked risk behaviours: Peter has had multiple partners, has been a sex worker, is faced with cultural and religious intolerance in his community, has had partners that weren't educated about safe sex, and has had his access to healthcare restricted by both the stigma surrounding his sexuality and his HIV. Moreover, his risk of contracting tuberculosis was exponentially higher because he lives, or lived, in Manenberg, an area where the disease is more prevalent, and his tik addiction made it more likely that he would engage in risky sexual behaviour. In fact, had I read the research before meeting him, I could have maybe, in Holmesian style, deduced everything about him before he even had a chance to tell me. I am glad I did not read the research because then I may never have really met him.

It is a wonder, I think to myself now, that he is sitting in front of me at all.

It was Pride Shelter that saved his life, for a time, and now he is hoping it will do so again. When I meet him, he is in the midst of his second stay there in so many years.

What happened?

He shrugs. 'After my first stay I went to rehab and it got better for a while. But then I fell off the wagon. I got back together with Frans, moved in with him. You know.'

After his relapse, he couldn't afford to go anywhere else; the Cape

Flats were where he had always lived. He was unemployed and a drug addict. Cape Town had already swallowed him in and spat him back out. He could not live on the streets again.

Though he was no longer on the streets, had moved back to the Cape Flats and had regular contact with his family again, things only got worse. Rehab had not worked and his meth habit could not live alongside his HIV. He was diagnosed with tuberculosis in his one lung three times within the space of a year.

That lung is now barely functioning.

He was also arrested for possession and received a five-year suspended sentence. He is convinced the judge assigned to his case, who he regards as an angel of mercy, gave him his second chance. 'She told me that I was too old to learn my lesson in jail. She said a fine wouldn't deter me either. So, she gave me that sentence. It was a warning: get arrested again and you'll get ten years, but for now we'll let you go.'

But it wasn't his health or his run-in with the law that finally convinced him he needed to make a change. It was God. 'There is religion on every street corner [in the Cape Flats], living right alongside gangsterism, and I found it,' he tells me earnestly.

THE PROPHET

On the day Denise finds Peter in the rain, she introduces him to a prophet.

It is a wet day, and the grey streets of Manenberg are empty because of the rain. Peter has left the house to escape Frans's rage and is wandering aimlessly down the street. Walking from the opposite direction, he sees Denise. He hurries towards her.

'What's wrong?' she asks immediately. Denise is an old friend of Frans's, and she has intimate knowledge of their affair. She knows theirs is a house plagued by drugs and violence, and she has made it a point to visit them once a week to give them spiritual guidance.

'Frans hit me again,' Peter says, 'I've had enough.'

The day Peter met Denise, she gave him the longest, truest hug he had ever received, and he became convinced it was a sign of something to come.

'Come on,' Denise says now, 'I am going to introduce to you someone who will lead you to the Lord.' Denise takes him by the hand and leads him into the heart of the neighbourhood.

Peter is led to a house and shown inside. Once there, he is introduced to Devon.

Devon wordlessly beckons for Peter to follow him. Devon is tall and muscular, a dominating presence. He is wearing a vest, pyjama bottoms and slippers. Tattoos spill out from his clothes onto his chest and arms. Peter can read these signs as well as anyone: this guy is the leader of the 27s, one of the most notorious prison gangs in South African history. But there is something magnetic about him, something in the way he listens to you. His silence is captivating and his eyes are soft. Peter immediately feels at ease. He tells Devon his life story, tells him about every sin he has ever committed.

When Peter has finished, the gang leader is silent.

He shows Peter his palms. Despite the wet, chilly day, they are covered in sweat. This, says Devon, is what your story has done to me. My sweat is a sign from God. My sweat is your anointing. He places his wet palms on Peter's face.

Devon tells Peter that he was visited by an angel that morning; the angel appeared before him and recited Psalm 23.

> The Lord is my shepherd; I shall not want. He maketh me to lie down in green pastures; he leadeth me beside the still waters. He restoreth my soul; he leadeth me in the paths of righteousness for his name's sake.

That had been a sign. That had been the voice of God.

'You are God sent,' Devon tells him. He baptises Peter right then and there.

It is a significant moment for Peter. In that room he feels purified, blessed. As if the skies could open and wash him in heavenly light.

'People who don't have faith might not have believed him, but I did,' Peter says when he tells me this story. Peter grew up in the constraints of the NG Kerk and had not really considered himself a religious person. 'I've always had issues with the church.

'But I suppose I have always been aware of my spirit-man, some other power. I've always known there was a God. But because of my flesh, because I wanted to experience things, I ignored it.'

Peter and I spend a lot of time together over the four weeks I visit Pride Shelter writing this story. I know he has withheld things, obscured things and perhaps lied to me. His story has gaps, holes that I am desperate to fill, and he often dances deftly around these, without filling them in. Still, don't we all do that? Dodge and dance and leave out what we must and say what we can?

Peter has always been willing to talk about sensitive issues; about things that I am sure must be difficult to confront and to deal with: being homeless, being a prostitute, being an addict, being the victim of rape and living with HIV. He has never raised his voice, been upset by a question or shown excess emotion. He is always calm, at times jovial and at times solemn, but always calm and always open.

But on our final afternoon, when I ask him about religion, he breaks down.

'I know that whatever I've done to myself – the abuse, the substances – I've done that to my body, not to the real me. The sexual abuse that happened to my body didn't happen to me. And even though I have the scars, I know that my spirit is intact. When I look at myself and I see what I've done to myself and what other people have done to me, I find it so strange that I can see past it,' he whispers slowly. He has tears rolling down his cheeks, over the bruise that still hasn't quite faded. 'I know that at some point I will leave this body behind and go to a better place and that makes me want to go on with life.'

He stops. He is sobbing and can no longer speak. I need to come back later.

A WORK IN PROGRESS

The day is warm and bright.

A middle-aged woman with bushy brown curls looks at me from the balcony and smiles. A cigarette is dangling from her lips.

'*Ek wil nie met jou praat nie* [I don't want to talk to you]' she shouts. She knows who I am and what I try to do here every week. But she laughs and tells me Peter will be right down.

Today, Peter and I are allowed to move our conversation from the kitchen to the inner sanctum of the ballroom turned AA meeting hall. Dereck, the elderly caretaker, drifts in and out, busy with his chores. The two dogs follow him around, panting softly. They are strays that the house took in a few years ago. A cockatoo watches with beady eyes from Dereck's shoulder and drops large white stains onto the back of his shirt. He doesn't seem to mind – or notice. Laundry is scattered across the room.

Peter has to move out by the end of the week. He talks about his future. At our previous meetings, he has always been optimistic about this topic, filled to the brim with life-affirming platitudes and assurances that God will ensure he is taken care of. 'There are a lot of things that I don't know. I struggle with things every day. I know things will come full circle. People are just people. People are all the same. We all want to be loved.'

But he is much less optimistic today. As soon as he sits down, he folds onto himself. He is crestfallen: things have not gone as well as he had hoped. He had applied for a temporary disability grant, but despite his legitimate respiratory problems, it has been denied. He can't, or won't, tell me why. He hasn't found a job like he hoped and he hasn't found a place to live.

Can't he stay at Pride Shelter given the circumstances? 'No,' he says, 'I need to move on.'

Before his first stay in Pride Shelter, while he was funding his meth habit with prostitution, living on the streets of Cape Town, he frequented a night shelter in Woodstock. Moira Henderson House, one of several Haven homeless shelters in Cape Town, is nothing like Pride Shelter and so much more like what I expected a homeless shelter to be. Like Pride Shelter, it is painted a bright yellow, the rules are the same and you have access to the same basic services.

But I understand why Pride Shelter is a better option. It feels like a home. It has a quiet domesticity that gives it a bright, restorative power. There is a matron and a caretaker that cut convincing mother and father figures: they are kindly and supportive. There are pets to love and take care of. Situated in the depth of middle-class suburbia, it is the kind of house that could, despite the torment and fear that it sheltered, allow you to dream. And it offers those dreams protection from the outside world. It is the kind of house where someone can be healed. The people who live inside it, who have suffered the horrors of abuse and persecution and were forced to flee, are given a chance to forget those horrors – at least for a time. Their surroundings do not constantly remind them how destitute they are. Quite the opposite – it gives them space to plan a better future and remember who they can be without the identity-crippling horrors of abuse and homelessness. Other shelters confront you with your reality. Pride Shelter is much subtler. It is one of Pride Shelter's founding philosophies to turn away from institutionalism, to be as small a presence in the lives of its occupants as possible. Pride Shelter wants to offer just that: shelter.

And, of course, Pride Shelter is also in a better position to refer LGBTI individuals to counsellors and health practitioners who can cater to their specific needs, without judgement or persecution, which is why the need for this kind of shelter was identified in the first place.

This space has allowed Peter to recoup parts of himself he had lost in the mire of drugs and abuse and homophobia. 'It's nice to get up and know I am in a safe space. I can't say I am happy, but I am content here, at peace,' he said when we first met.

After he left Pride Shelter the first time he lived here, he was hopeful and inspired. He even briefly got a job at a charity organisation called Reach for Life. He was drug-free; he had a purpose. But the chaos dragged him back down again and brought him to his knees.

And now, once again, he finds himself facing the real world. What happens when he enters places that do not make it so easy to be himself? This time, what will he do in the face of the chaos?

Will he go back to rehab? No, he can't afford it.

Is he currently seeking counselling or attending AA meetings?

'No,' he says. He hasn't attended one since he has moved into the house. 'There is one here tonight. I might go. But come this afternoon, who knows? I'll go if God wants me to.'

Has he been back to church since he left Manenberg?

He has not attended a single church service or sought out the help of any other spiritual leader, but he reads the Bible every day.

'I'll be fine,' he tells me. 'I have faith, I have God. Everything will work out. If something doesn't make sense to me, I just let it go. If I can't figure it out, I don't break my mind over it. If God wants me to, you know, figure it out, he will reveal it to me. I'm really not that hard on myself anymore. Um, I used to be. I used to be really anxious.'

What about his daughter? Will he see her?

She lives with her mother and stepfather now. Peter hasn't seen her in a while, but they speak regularly. He says he doesn't want to burden her with his problems, but anticipates that he will have to have a difficult conversation with her soon. 'Thank God she's really mature. She's like my sister,' he says wryly. 'In fact, she's like my mother.'

Is he going to try getting back in touch with Reach for Life or another charity organisation?

He might. He wants to help people and he sees his experiences as a kind of horrible gift given to him by God: to be able to stop other people from making the same mistakes that he has made and to be able to help gay people in his community would be a blessing.

'I would love to give back. I would love to serve people. I would love to help in any capacity. Whether it is cleaning toilets or being president,' he laughs. 'You can only enjoy so much in the flesh,' he says, looking serious. 'I have put so many chemicals in my body, and yet I can still string a sentence together,' he is almost reverential. 'There's always a way out. I'm alive and I'm here today and I have a chance.'

We are interrupted by one of the other housemates, who wants to go down to the local internet café. Peter is going with him; he wants to go look for a job.

This will be our last meeting.

I walk out with them, unsure about how I feel about this house and how much permanent change it can really affect.

Peter seems to sense my dissatisfaction. 'Don't worry about me,' he says, seemingly back to his old cheerful self. 'I used to mess up a lot. I'm still not where I want to be. But I'll be fine.

'I am a work in progress.'

Wednesdays are trash days in Oranjezicht. Peter leaves me standing on the curb. Next to me there are two homeless boys searching through the refuse they have rescued from the house's bins. Together, we watch Peter disappear down the street. The afternoon shadow of Table Mountain stretches out in front of him like dark angelic wings.

* The names of the people in this story have been changed to protect their identities.

Dean's bed

DEAN HUTTON

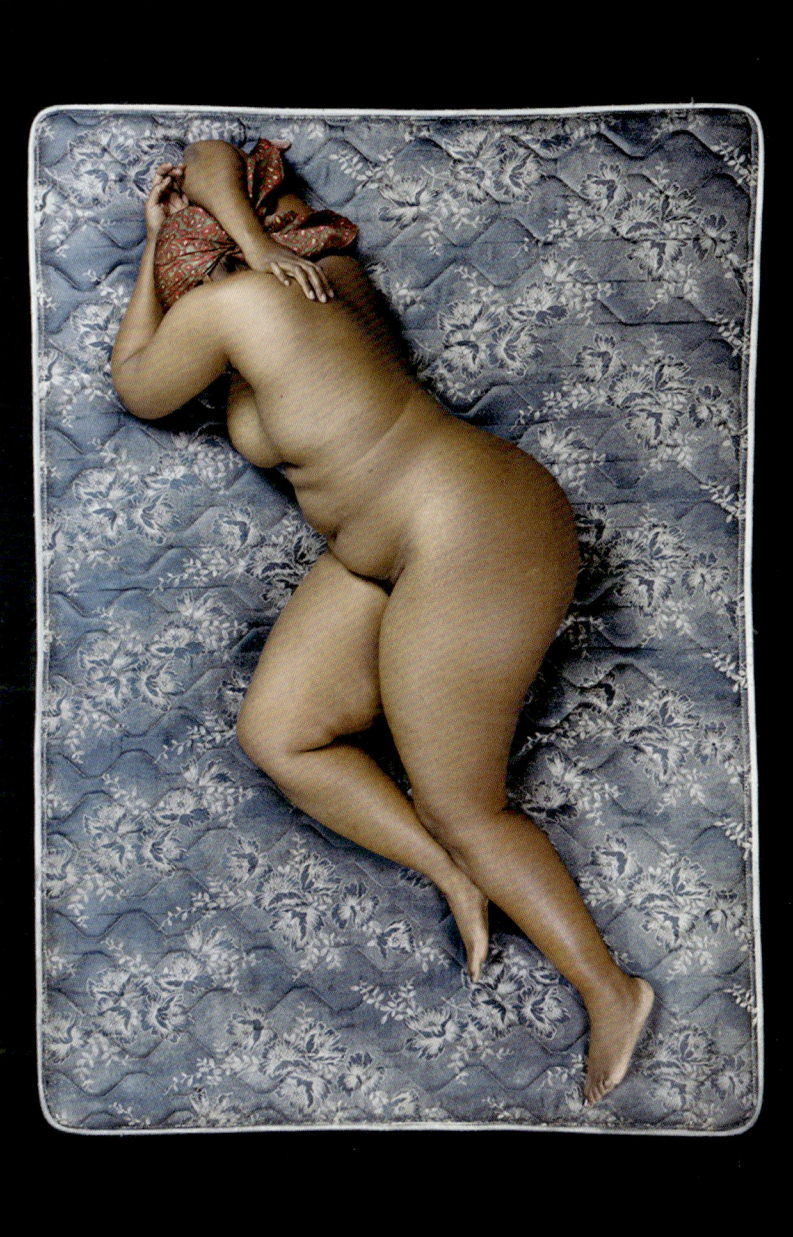

Melissa

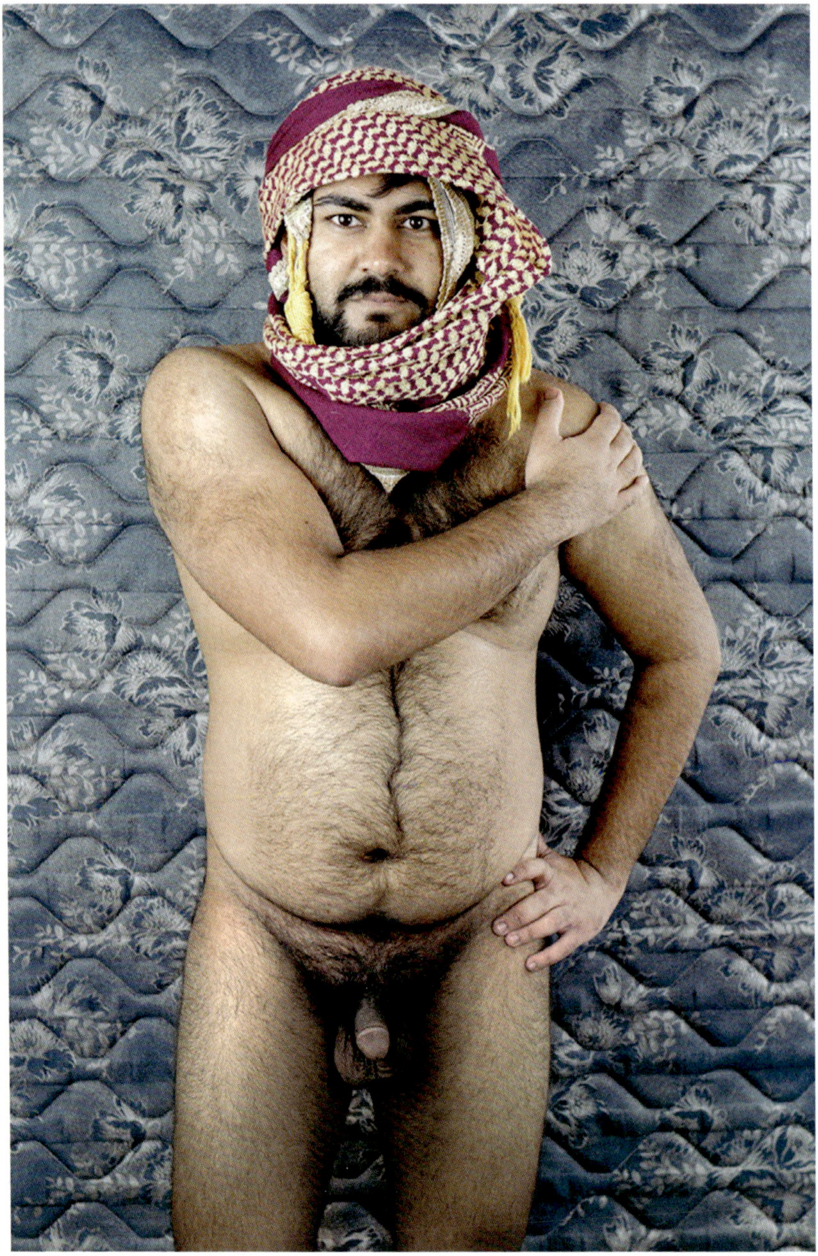

Gabriel

Lesley   Sonia

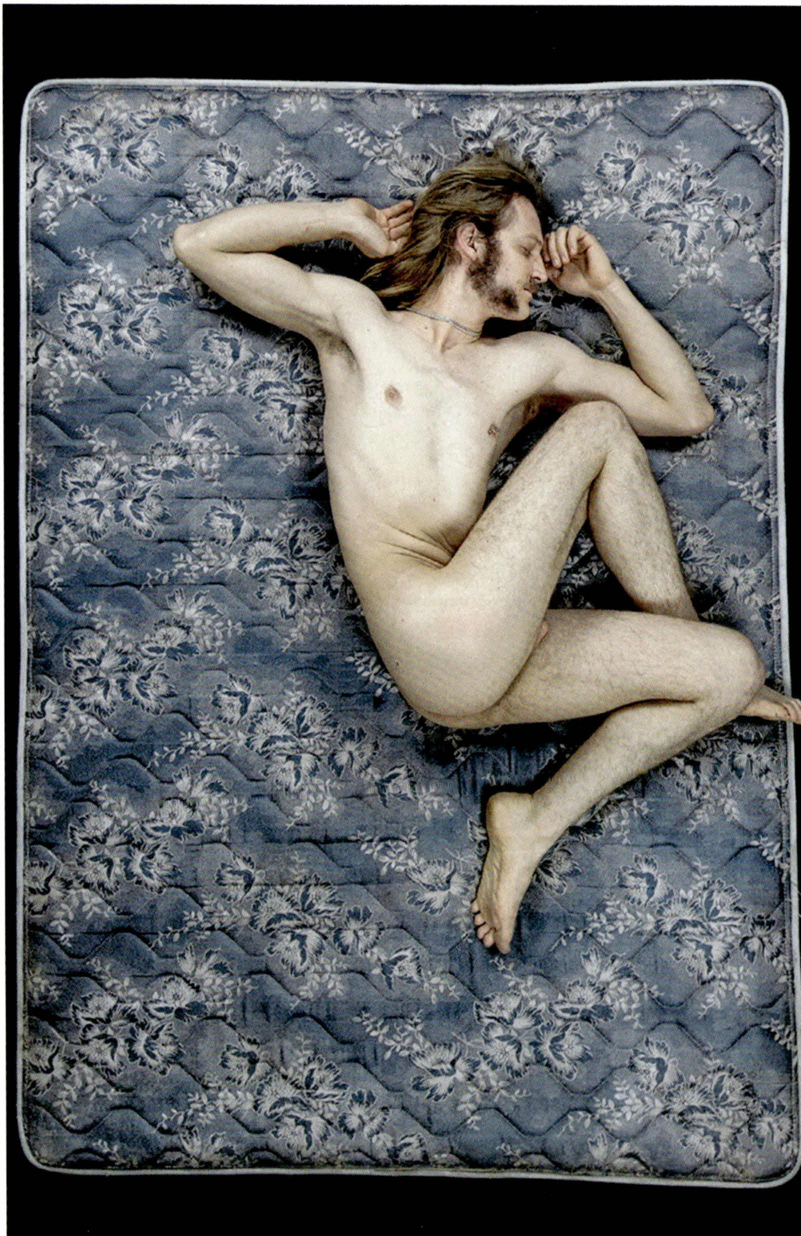

Benjamin

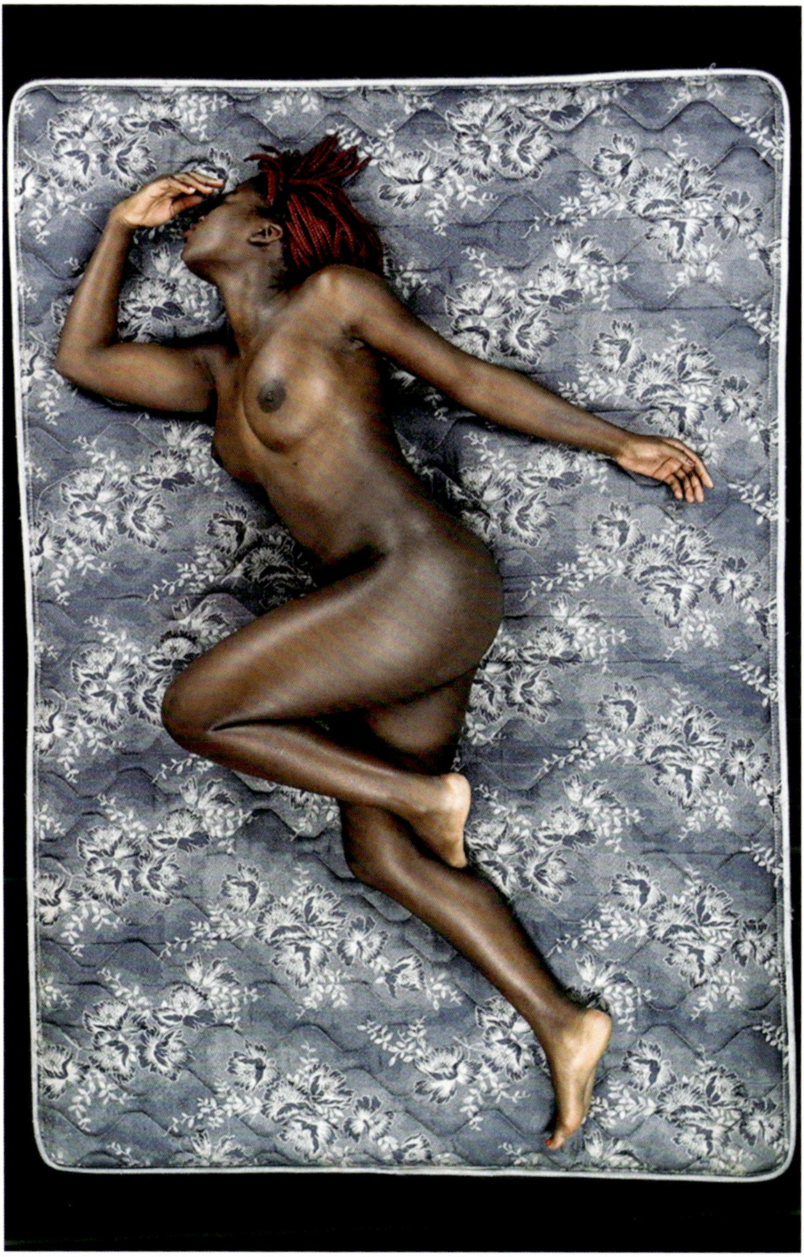

Tokologo

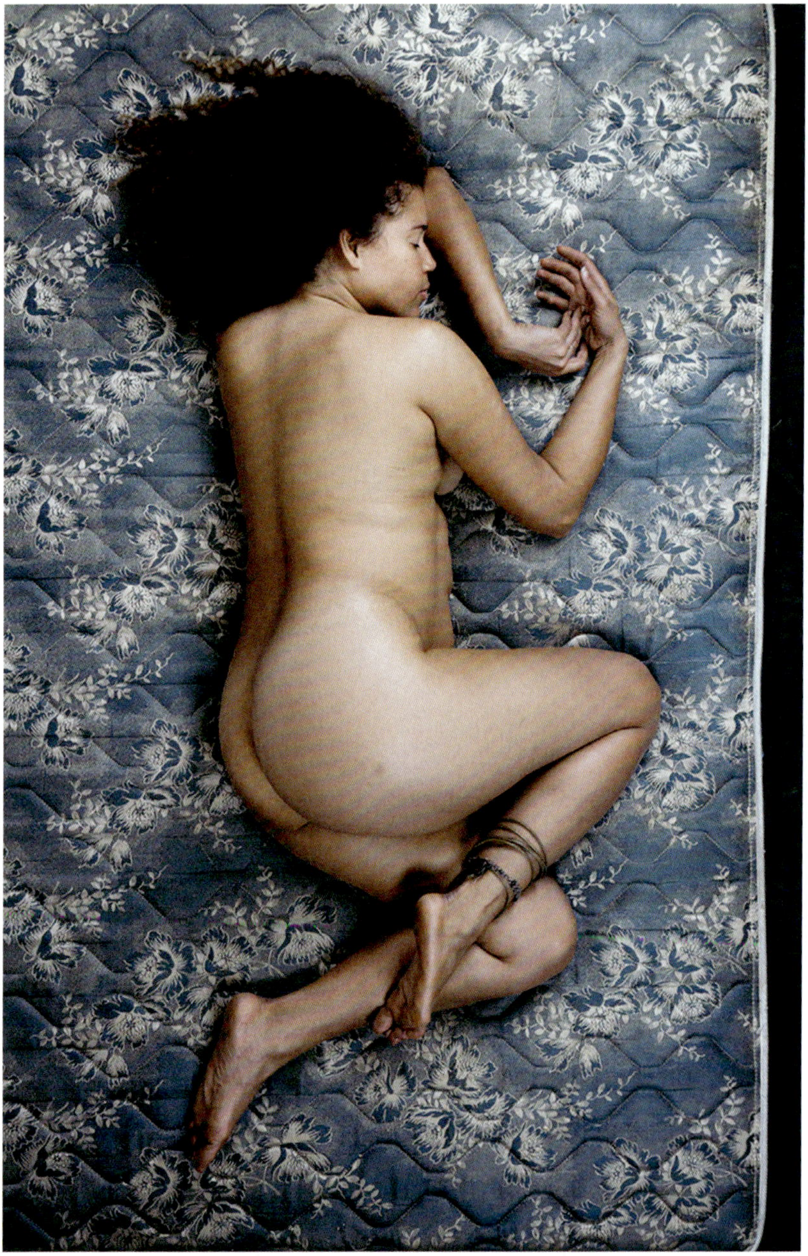

Alberta

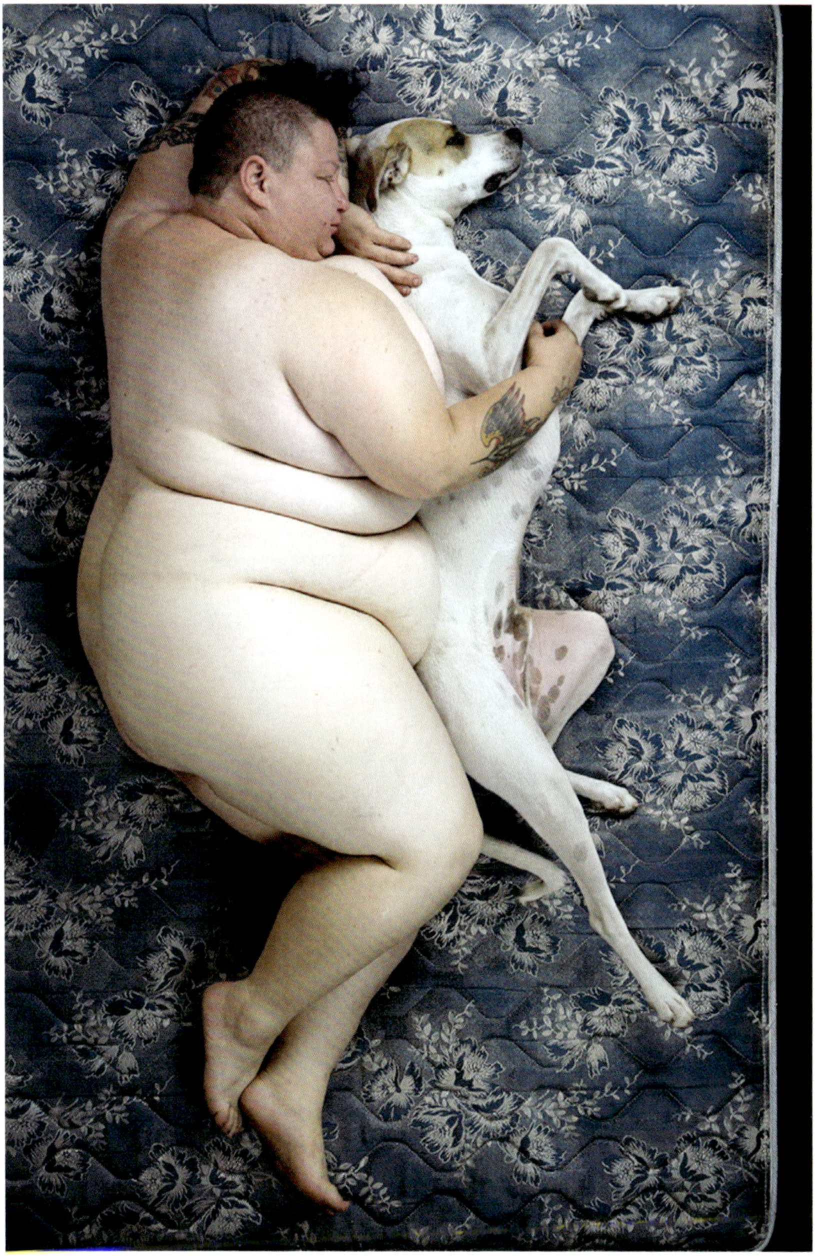

Dean

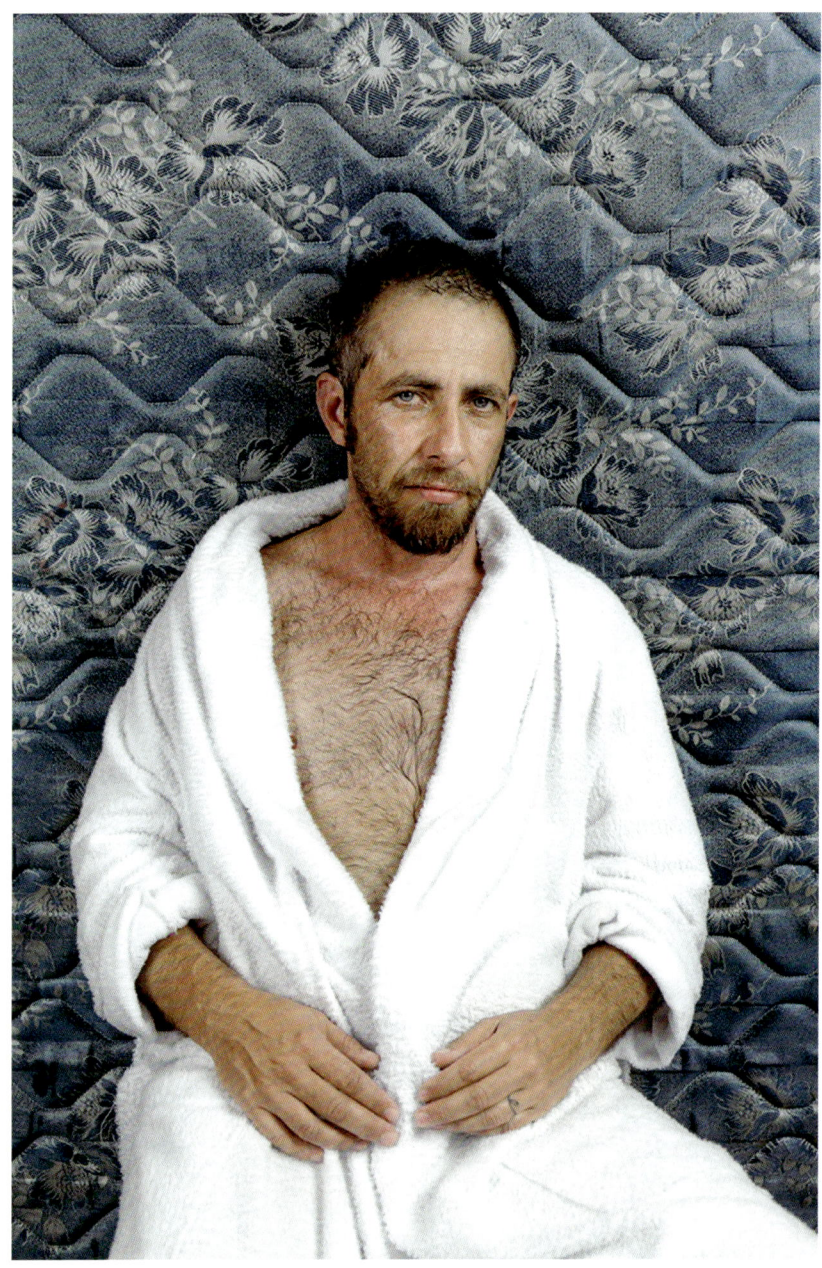

Robert

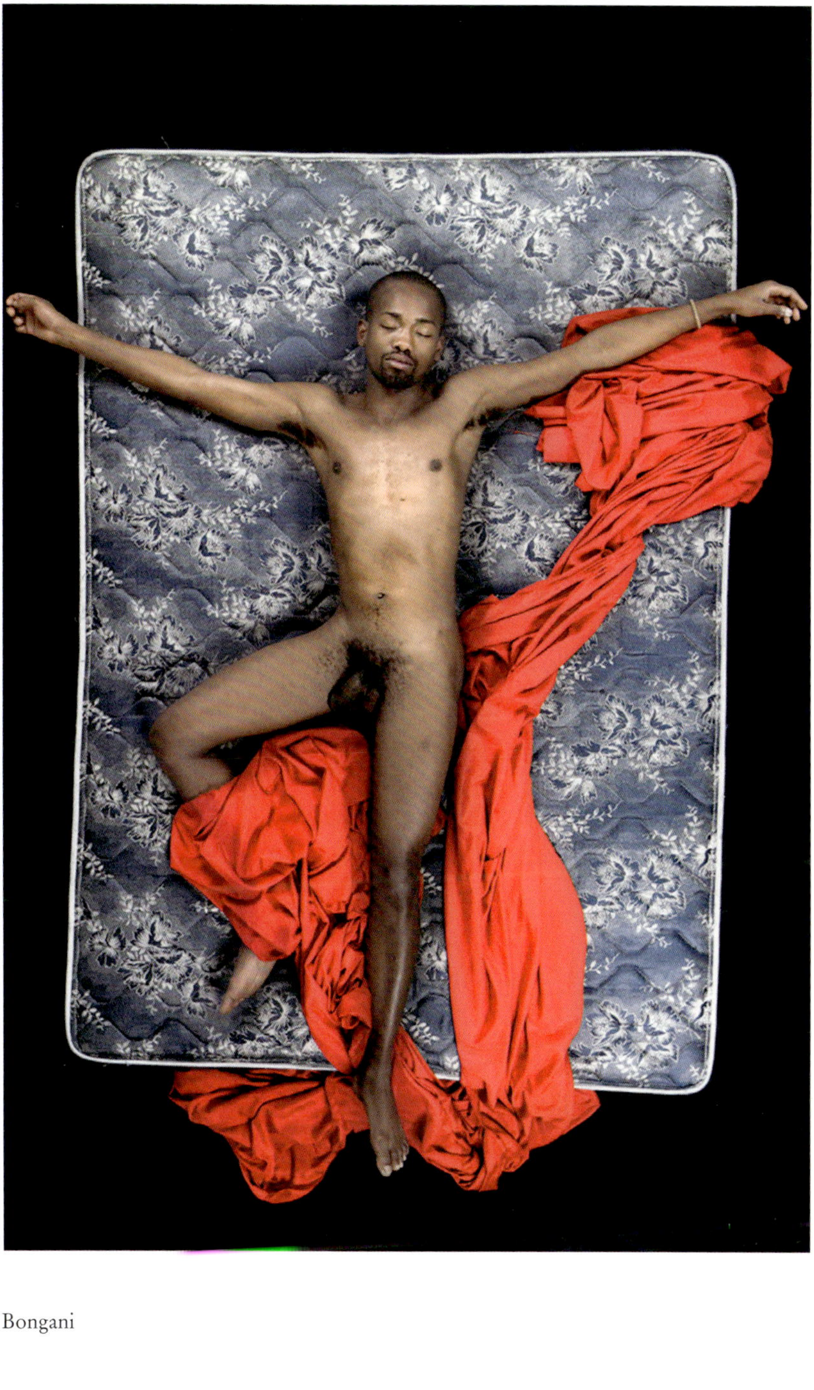

Bongani

Midnight in Lusikisiki
or
(The ruin of the gentlewomen)

SINDISWA BUSUKU-MATHESE

One by one, the old womenfolk appear. Each falls to her knees in a field of mud. Floral pinafores flapping in the wind. Rain rolls down their faces and into their eyes. They are draped in black shawls. The trees above are creaking. They turn to look at each other. The field has turned to blood. They whisper into each other's hands, 'Cover me with a veil. Evening has collapsed.' After a long silence they climb to their feet. Then the womenfolk begin to walk backwards. A fluorescent swarm of fireflies rises agile in the sky. Each woman scatters in a separate direction. Each disappears into the tall maize. All of them waving and smiling so broadly their lips begin to crack. The field has turned to bone.

Soon they begin to laugh uncontrollably through their tears and their blood-stained teeth, whispering, 'Lonmin has hollowed out our aching bodies.'

Two weddings for Amoit

DILMAN DILA

AMOIT SAT ON A THREE-LEGGED STOOL, peeling *matooke* for lunch. Sweat gleamed on her skin although an air con hummed from the wall. She whistled a tune from a folk song about a man wrongfully accused of stealing chickens and, aware of Aceng's eyes on her, she shook her shoulders in a dance. She tried not to smile, pretending not to notice Aceng's ogling, but she couldn't fight it anymore. She looked up, their eyes met, and they both smiled. For the first time since their wedding, they were alone.

They married a month ago without any funfair, without the colourful ceremonies that their ancestors performed during *Nyumba Nthobu* weddings. They had simply walked up to the marriage registrar and signed papers. The next day Amoit had welcomed Aceng into her home with a cake and a red rose. There had been no kiss, no hug, no display of emotions, not even a shake of hands, even though fires blazed through their veins and threatened to overwhelm them.

'Welcome,' Amoit had said.

'Thank you,' Aceng had replied.

'We shall look after you well,' Amoit's husband, Omongo, had said. He had stood beside Amoit at the doorway, smiling too hard, holding a white rose.

'Thank you,' Aceng had said, taking both flowers.

On the coffee table, beside the new issue of *Christian Living Today*, there were more papers to sign – personal terms of the marriage, like how much time Aceng could spend alone with their mutual husband and how Aceng would relate to the babies she would produce for them – which the registrar did not need to be part of. No one had said a word as they signed the papers. Then Amoit had sliced the cake and poured mango juice into three glasses.

'You are now my wife,' Amoit had said, raising her glass in a toast.

'I'm honoured to serve you both,' Aceng had replied, raising her glass.

'Here's to a fertile marriage,' Omongo had said.

The three had clinked glasses and drank the juice. The two women took tiny sips. Omongo drained his glass in a long swig and then slammed it onto the table.

'I'm a good man,' he said to Aceng. 'You are my now my wife's wife, and I don't know what to call you, so I'll call you my sister-in-law. I won't force myself on to you unless –'

'There's no need for a speech,' Aceng had said, cutting him short with a smile.

Amoit and Aceng never got time to be alone in the days that followed. Omongo was always present. The planting season had just ended and because the agrobots took care of tending the maize, getting rid of weeds and pests, watering, and spraying fertilisers and growth enhancers, there was little for him to do in the garden. He spent a bit of time monitoring the robots, but other than that he was home reading his Bible and poring over literature the government sent every day. Now, a month later, the crops would soon be ready for harvest. For the next two weeks he would hardly find any time away from the garden. He would have to prepare the granaries, hire harvesters, find a buyer and then prepare for the next round of planting. He would be away from home most of the day and this would give the two women a perfect opportunity to be alone. Because it was Saturday Amoit did not have to go to court and Aceng was not expected at school. They had the house to themselves.

A mischievous light twinkled in Aceng's eyes. She looked out the window to make sure there was no one in the backyard, and then she drew the curtains. The room darkened. She then peeped out of the back door to be sure that the yard was empty before pulling the door shut. They lived in a suburb of little bungalows, with wall fences about four-feet high enclosing each home, so it wasn't strange for a neighbour to pop over to borrow a pinch of salt, or a bit of sugar, or this or that. Besides, they had the only backyard flower garden in the street, which meant neighbours were always climbing over the wall to pick roses. Some neighbours had become so friendly that they didn't have to ask before plucking a few flowers.

Finally, Aceng closed the inner door that led to the living room and the rest of the house. The only light came from the solar stove; its blue glow cast a cold ambiance that contrasted with the warmth flowing between the two women. Aceng smiled, showing off the gap between her front teeth and the deep dimple on her right cheek. These were the two traits that had drawn Amoit to her. Amoit wore a *lesu*, the ends of which were tied behind her neck. She undid the knot and the cloth slipped off. Her nipples were long. Her chocolate skin gleamed with sweat and caught the light of the stove, creating the illusion of blue icing on a cake. Aceng knelt between her legs and they kissed.

Their first kiss after marriage.

They had kissed a lot before the wedding, but always in hiding, in dark places at the park, in the toilets where there were no cameras. Only once had they made love – in Amoit's hall at Makerere University during a rare power outage. Rumour had it the saboteurs had blown up a microwave transmitter, but everyone dismissed this as idle gossip. After all, who would want to sabotage a Christian utopia? Amoit and Aceng took advantage of the blackout, for it meant the security cameras in the hall were dead. Amoit's three roommates were not in the dorm at the time, so they made love quickly. They had come at the same instant, as though their bodies were already accustomed to one another.

Now they were married. There were no cameras in the house, no one to run into them but Amoit's husband. They finally had time to savour their love.

It was not to be. The hum of a bruka blared into the kitchen, growing louder each second. They stopped kissing and listened. They did not expect Omongo back before noon. That might be a neighbour's ornithopter. Still, they had to be careful. Though Omongo loved Amoit, he loved his Bible more and if he caught them he would send them to the firing squad.

The bruka hovered right overhead, preparing to land on the roof pad. It had to be Omongo. The sound of the flying machine intensified. Shaped like an egg with a pair of wings on the top and painted a wine red, the bruka was Omongo's favoured mode of transportation. It was him – they could hear it as the door slid open. The women jumped apart. Amoit fumbled to tie the *lesu*, cursing. Aceng yanked the curtains open, flooding the kitchen with sunlight, and then pushed open the back door. Amoit resumed peeling bananas while Aceng washed dishes at the sink.

A few moments later, Omongo ran in. He had a smile on his face, the same smile that had graced his and Amoit's wedding day a little over a year ago. The smile had vanished six months later when a doctor told them Amoit was barren. A frown had smothered his face since then, and it had deepened as he sank into debt. His garden had thrice failed to yield. The reappearance of the smile could only mean good news. Amoit's first thought was that the garden had done very well, which would allow him pay off all his debts.

'Yes!' Omongo said, punching the air.

'What happened?' Amoit said, getting to her feet.

'Yes! Yes! Yes!' he screamed. He hugged her so tight that she couldn't breathe. She shoved him away gently, disentangling from his embrace. His smile widened, showing off his yellowish teeth. 'We don't need her anymore,' he said, breathless.

'You are not making sense,' Amoit said.

'We don't need her anymore,' Omongo said in a whisper, as though he did not want Aceng to overhear. He did not look at Aceng as he spoke. 'You'll have to divorce her.'

* * *

Half a century ago, the drought they called The Big Burn had reduced the population by half. It left famine and disease in its wake. Though the country had recovered, the population continued to decline. Still today, fifty years later, one in four women is barren, has suffered miscarriages or has given birth to stillborn babies.

According to the Christian Council, which had become very powerful in the wake of The Big Burn, God was still angry with humanity. Although the Council had succeeded in creating a Christian utopia out of the ashes of the drought, its leaders were adamant that there were still sinners in their midst. God would continue to punish them with population decline until the sinners repented. In another one hundred years their great country would be no more – unless everyone became holy.

Science failed to help. No medicine could cure barren women. No quality of medical care could stop miscarriages and stillbirths, the causes of which were unknown. Some scientists speculated that infertility was a side effect of the geoengineering that had been necessary to fight The Big Burn. Others argued it was due to the reliance on chemical foods to fight famine. There had been multiple attempts at cloning as a solution, but the babies had so many defects that they spent ninety per cent of their short lives in hospitals. Most died before their fifth birthdays.

As a response, the Christian Council permitted polygamy. They cited the case of Abraham and Sarah as a sign of Biblical approval, and they revived an ancient custom, *Nyumba Nthobu*, in which a barren woman could marry another woman to bear children on her behalf. The woman she married would be her wife and perform all the normal duties of a wife – except making love. They insisted this custom provided evidence that East Africans were the Jews of the Bible. They drew a direct line to Sarah, who urged Abraham to sleep with her maid Hagar so she could have the children God promised her. To avoid promiscuity, once Sarah married Hagar, she would never divorce her. The twist the Christian Council introduced was that in light of the birthing crisis, a modern-day Sarah could lend a modern-day Hagar to other childless couples once Hagar was proven to be successfully fertile. Husbands were not allowed to lend out their wives and, in fact, they had a duty to prevent homosexuality within their marriages. The Council was at pains to emphasise that the arrangement was purely entered into for procreation, not for lustful purposes. If the police found Sarah and Hagar to be lesbians and the husband didn't report them, then all three would face the firing squad.

* * *

Amoit had fallen in love with Aceng during a church choir practice while still at university. Their deep Christian upbringing told them it was a sin; one of the sins that caused God to punish the country with a declining population. Still, they could not resist temptation. They met in secret, in the toilets, in dark places, for only a few seconds, to relish in the desire they had for each other. They knew there were others like them, sinners living in secret Sodoms and Gomorrahs. They searched until they found an underground group, unsurprisingly called Survivors of Gomorrah. There they learned how to enjoy their love right under the nose of the Christian Council. There were many tricks. The favourite was *Nyumba Nthobu*. Once this pathway was opened up to them, Amoit seduced Omongo and they got married. Amoit consulted a doctor in the group who certified her as barren, and with this certificate she convinced Omongo to allow her to find a Hagar.

'But we need children,' Amoit said. 'How can we get rid of her if I can't have children?'

'Science saves the day,' Omongo said.

He pulled out his iSnic and showed her the headline: 'Breakthrough in Reproductive Health'. For decades, scientists had tried to use the knowledge God gave them to ensure the survival of the country. They succeeded in genetic engineering of crops and splicing species to create new breeds, but they had failed to address population decline. Until now. Finally they had successfully managed to create an artificial womb by using cells from the endotrium. They called the technology New Sera, and it not only prevented miscarriages, stillbirths and premature births, it also solved infertility and made conceiving using cloned sperms and eggs a more efficient process.

'Oh –' Amoit started to groan, but remembered that she was supposed to be happy. 'Yay,' she said. 'But –'

'It works perfectly for us,' Omongo said.

'Yes it does,' Amoit said. 'But the Bible does not allow divorce.'

'Well,' Omongo said, 'the Council will grant us a divorce license. It won't be a sin.'

He showed her a paragraph in the article. It said that sixteen women and four men had been executed for homosexuality in the previous year – up from six women and no men the year before. This, according to the police, indicated that some people were abusing *Nyumba Nthobu* and, as they now had New Sera, the Christian Council will have to annul *Nyumba Nthobu*. He read aloud: 'All Iagars will have the right to leave with their children, seeing that barren women can now have children of their own.' The article ended on an ambiguous note, stating that New Sera was still a very expensive technology and not everybody would be able to afford it. What would annulling marriages mean for the poor?

'Ask her if she is pregnant,' Omongo said.

Amoit wondered why he could not talk directly to Aceng. She turned to Aceng, but she could not look into her eyes for fear that it would betray their relationship.

'Are you pregnant?' Amoit ask her.

'No,' Aceng said. 'I bled this morning.'

'Good,' Omongo said. 'The divorce will be easy.'

Amoit clung to the hope that New Sera would be too expensive. Though the government would offer subsidies to ensure as many women as possible bore children, each pregnancy would cost a hundred thousand shillings. In future, the technology might become more affordable that it could become a free government programme, but the scientists quoted said it would not happen anytime soon. Omongo was already in debt to the tune of five hundred thousand shillings. He inherited the garden from his father, who had used natural seeds to grow crops, but of late the Christian Council had decreed that all farmers use genetically engineered seeds, which were manufactured by a corporation called B-Gete. The idea was to ensure that humanity did not fall victim to calamities like The Big Burn again. Survivors of Gomorrah were sceptical; many thought it was a secret mind-control programme. Who knew what drugs they were putting into the food supply?

Omongo had to buy B-Gete seeds with a terminator gene, which made it impossible to replant or keep a seed bank. However, B-Gete products were magical: they matured in only one month, which guaranteed farmers quick returns. Despite this, Omongo had failed to make a profit since switching from natural seeds. The last three harvests had been so dismal that he had had to borrow money to buy new seeds each time he wanted to plant. Neither B-Gete nor the Department of Agriculture could give him a proper explanation for the failed harvests.

'There might be a sin in your life,' an officer from the Department of Agriculture had told him. 'God might be withholding the harvest to tell you to look carefully at your life. Maybe it is because you don't have children?'

It was after this that Omongo had agreed to allow a Hagar into their family. He had wanted to obey God's command of going forth and multiplying.

At the same time he had followed the advice of B-Gete and gone fully mechanical. He got a loan to buy agrobots and, although his debt increased, he no longer had to pay workers. The agrobots looked after his garden more efficiently than any human could, monitoring the growth of each and every plant with meticulous precision. They had generated daily reports, which made him anticipate a bounty harvest.

* * *

'Can we afford it?' Amoit had asked.

Even with good harvests it would take Omongo five years to clear his debts. Another two years would be required to afford New Sera. Amoit's salary, at a gross of ten thousand a year, was negligible. They could not count on it.

'I have done everything by the book. A B-Gete official has been checking the agrobots every few days. I married a Hagar to have children. What more can I do? To the best of my knowledge, everything is right in the garden and everything is right between me and God. I will have a bounty harvest and will be on my feet in a year. All this I declare in the name of Jesus.'

'Amen,' Amoit said.

'I bind those demons that have been frustrating my garden. I claim a bounty harvest in the name of Jesus!' Omongo went down on his knees and burst into a fervent prayer. He cast out demons, asking God to bless his garden, asking forgiveness for whatever crimes he had committed but did not know about. Omongo pleaded with God to remove the curse on his garden. Amoit went on her knees with him, and after a few moments Aceng joined them. The prayer went on for twenty minutes. By which time, Amoit's knees were hurting and she was silently praying that God would shut up her husband. Her prayers were answered. 'God I know you've heard my cry,' Omongo concluded. 'I know you'll open the door for me.'

'Amen,' Amoit said.

They stood up. Omongo kissed her, and then said to Aceng, 'I'm sorry,' and walked out.

Amoit waited until she heard him going up the stairs to the roof pad, and then she hugged Aceng and kissed her on the lips.

'We'll find a way,' she said.

Amoit ran after Omongo and caught up with him just as he turned the ignition on the bruka. The craft hummed in preparation for takeoff. Omongo slid open the door.

'It might be a good idea to make her pregnant …' she said.

'Are you scared we won't afford it?'

'No,' she said. 'I have faith that God will answer our prayers, but New Sera is a beta tech. Anything can go wrong. It might not deliver as efficiently as promised. All I'm saying is that, since we have this opportunity, we should try to use it.'

'I don't like sleeping with her,' Omongo said.

'We still have to follow God's word,' Amoit said. 'We have to multiply. Let's not throw away this chance until New Sera takes a firm root.'

He was silent for several moments. 'It tortures me every time I look at her,' he said.

'I know,' Amoit said. 'I pray every day for God to open up my womb the way he did for Sarah, so that you don't have to go through all this.'

'I love you,' he finally said.

They kissed. She broke off too soon, but he did not protest. He closed the door and the bruka jumped into the air. She watched until the ornithopter vanished along the horizon, thinking that if Aceng got pregnant they would have two more years together. That was enough time to make an alternative plan. She felt sorry for Omongo for using him. He was a fanatic Christian who believed The Big Burn and the ensuing great famine and diseases were signs of the End of Times and that the rapture would happen soon, taking all pure Christians to their true home in heaven. While she respected his right to believe in these things, she was tired of their implications. Amoit thought that it was people like Omongo who had caused The Big Burn. By insisting that earth was not home, that home was somewhere else and that *their* God gave them dominion over earth, they behaved in ways that destroyed it. She knew she could have been executed for having such thoughts, but she couldn't help it.

From childhood she had been taught that The Big Burn, the great famine, the epidemics, the floods and the wars were all the works of the Horsemen of the Apocalypse as foretold in Revelations. Then she read banned books, old books from way before the calamities started, and she understood what had happened. It was not the Horsemen. It was the actions of ordinary people – people like Omongo. They did not care about earth.

She went back to the kitchen and kissed Aceng again. She tried to continue from where her husband had interrupted, but the moment was gone and the danger of separation hung between them like a cloud of metallic particles.

'We should escape to Congo,' Aceng said. 'There has to be a way.'

Congo had beaten off all attempts by The Christian Utopia of East Africa to annex it. Though its economy and technology were inferior to those of East Africa and most of its people still lived in grass-thatched huts like prehistoric human beings, it had enough nuclear bombs to deter the Christian Council from attacking. Very little was known about Congo, because the Christian Council behaved as if it did not exist, but it was a favourite topic of the Survivors of Gomorrah. Many dreamed about sneaking across the border to that paradise. This would have been possible if the Christian Council had not built a laser wall around East Africa, making it impossible for its citizens to mix with the devil worshippers in Congo, or the false Christians in Ethiopia, or the Muslims in Sudan and Somalia. The only open border was with the Christian Utopia of South Africa. The only way to get to those other lands was via an underground network of tunnels. She had never seen any such tunnels but she had been told they existed.

'Let's cook,' Amoit said. 'I'm hungry.'

She returned to peeling potatoes. She thought about other strategies Survivors of Gomorrah used, like Birungi and Ankunda, who had both married men and had children yet met often to consummate their love. It seemed to be the best way to beat the system, though it meant not seeing each other every day. Sometimes they went for months without physical contact but at least they were bound together through their marriages. *Nyumba Nthobu* had seemed the perfect way for Amoit and Aceng to be together for the rest of their lives.

They had to stay together. Somehow. They could have a couple of years if Aceng got pregnant, or maybe a few months if Omongo's garden prospered. But if Omongo's garden failed, they could possibly get ten years, maybe more, until New Sera became cheap enough to be offered as a free service. It was clear to Amoit: the garden had to fail.

They cooked in silence. As Aceng mashed the *matooke*, Amoit called Omongo to return for lunch. He told her he was in the middle of interviewing harvesters, so he wouldn't be home until after six. They had to eat alone. They spread a mat on the kitchen floor and put the mashed bananas on a tray between them. Thick groundnut sauce, laced with *ntula* and strips of smoked fish, was in a bowl beside the *matooke*. They ate with their fingers.

Half way through the meal Amoit licked the sauce off Aceng's fingers, and before they knew what was happening, they were making love on the kitchen floor.

They lay in each other's arms for a long time, naked, their bodies glistening with sweat, aware that the back door and curtains were open, letting in a strong beam of sunlight. If a neighbour came hunting for flowers, they would be sent to the firing squad.

'I have to go to church,' Amoit said.

'To pray for Congo?' Aceng said.

'Yes,' Amoit said. 'Or an alternative.'

She dressed in a green *gomesi*, the Mother's Union uniform. Every married woman was required to wear it to church. As they owned only one bruka, which Omongo used, she rode a bicycle. A good thing about the *gomesi* was that it had solar-powered air conditioning to keep her cool as she cruised down the streets. Everyone was indoors, hiding away from the sun. Her suburb looked devoid of life, apart from the cleaning robots that darted up and down, chasing after dead leaves and grass. The only sound seemed to be the whirr of her bicycle as it rolled on the tarmac.

The church was a little red-brick structure with a huge white cross on the roof. It sat on top of a green hill, visible from three miles away. The hill was too steep for Amoit to ride, so she pushed the bicycle up to the church. From there, she had a grand view of the city; the skyscrapers seemed to jut out of a jungle. After The Big Burn, there had been a mad rush to reforest the land as geoengineers advised that a rapid increase in tree cover would reverse the effects of the Horsemen, and would fight back against Satan's attempt to kill Christians by changing the weather. They used genetically modified drought-resistant trees that matured within months, and within a few years the entire land was choked with trees.

One building stood out in the city's skyline – a red cylinder so tall its top was lost in the clouds, so big it looked like a mountain. In the middle was the B-Gete logo, the corporation on whose shoulder the Christian Council put the future of humanity.

Many years after reforestation, the heat had still not diminished. Farmers like Omongo were forced to grow crops in special domed gardens. The city looked empty with only a few brukas flying about like lost birds. Everyone else stayed indoors most of the time, afraid of the sun.

She turned off the air con that was built into her *gomesi* and stepped into the church, which was cool and protected from the sun. Its windows had coloured glass panes that cast rainbow beams onto the pews. A huge neon cross glowed behind the altar. A long time ago, according to some Survivors of Gomorrah, this had been a Catholic church full of statues of Jesus, Mary, the apostles and the saints. Now, there was no sign of any of that. After the Great Revival, which saw the Pentecostals sweeping into power and the Christian Council becoming the government, all other Christian sects were banned. Still, they had borrowed many customs from the ancient sects. Confession became a therapy session, with sinners encouraged to go to the pastor for psychiatric guidance. It no longer happened in booths, but in the

Pastor's Room, behind the altar. As Amoit stepped in, she noticed there were three people waiting to go to confession.

'Praise the Lord, brother and sisters,' Amoit said in greeting.

'Amen,' they chorused. 'God is good all the time.'

'And all the time God is good,' Amoit responded.

She sat in the queue and began reading her Bible, hoping none of them would engage her in small talk. She did not know any of them and she wasn't in the mood to make new friends.

Her turn came and she went into the Pastor's Room. It was spacious, with bare furnishings. Pastor sat behind a simple desk, which had nothing but a lamp and a Bible. He had a bald head, bulbous cheeks and a baby's smile.

'Good to see you, Amoit,' Pastor said. 'Praise the Lord.'

'Amen,' said Amoit, sitting on a leather chair at the other side of the desk. 'God is good all the time.'

'And all the time God is good,' Pastor replied. 'You look troubled.'

Pastor was one of the leaders in Survivors of Gomorrah. He and his lover had swapped partners with a lesbian couple. They all worked in the church, living in the same compound, and they had children. A perfect cover. It had been a lucky meeting for them. His partner was the treasurer while his wife was the choir master and her partner the chief usher.

'You heard about New Sera,' Amoit said, dropping her voice to a whisper. They had to take precautions in case someone was listening outside the door.

'Yes,' Pastor said. 'It's good news for us.'

'But bad news for some of us,' Amoit said. 'We have to go to Congo.'

Pastor shook his head. 'The tunnels were busted last year. There is rumour of a new one being dug, but it won't be ready for another five years and we pray they don't find it as well.'

'We can't live here anymore,' Amoit said.

'You have other options,' Pastor said. 'There's a new couple in town. We could match you and Aceng with them.'

That was good news indeed. It would be a perfect cover, better than *Nyumba Nthobu*. The only problem was that she was married to Omongo and could not remarry, unless she became a widow. She looked at the Pastor as this dawned on her. Surely he cannot be talking about her waiting until after her husband's death.

'It can be done,' the Pastor said, as though reading her mind. 'Just say yes and he will get a ticket to Heaven.'

Amoit frowned, not understanding what Pastor was talking about. She sensed it had something to do with violence, but she didn't want to allow her mind to wander down that path. She was born long after the Christian Council had created the utopia. She grew up in a world where the streets were paved with love, where every breath exhaled happiness – and where infertility was the only dark thing. All day long the TV showed angelic choirs singing praises to God, the news bulletins reported happy story after happy story, and the movies and programmes all glorified the paradise that was utopia. The TVs didn't show any violence, nor talk about it. In utopia there were no murders and no robberies. There was nothing but peace and harmony and love. It was impossible to imagine hunger because the Christian Council supplied free food, and there were no bills to pay because the government provided free water and energy. She could not imagine what crime meant, for she had never heard of it happening in real life. She knew about sin, but in her mind it involved things like homosexuality, telling lies, fornication and adultery. She sometimes heard of darker things in Survivors of Gomorrah gatherings, things like those that happened in the Bible, like the murder of Abel, but many things that happened in the Bible, such as people walking on water, no longer happened in the real world, so whenever she heard of anything dark, her mind brushed it off as a fairy tale.

She tried to concretise Pastor's words, but the only time a person's life could end was either by natural causes, an accident or through the firing squad – and the firing squad were angels in human form tasked with dispensing God's justice in the utopia.

She looked at her fingers, thinking about the day she met Omongo in a Bible study session at university. He was sitting beside a window at sunset, only half his face lit up, as he read from Psalms, 'The Lord is my light and my salvation, whom shall I fear?' His voice sounded like that of an actor on stage.

'If his crop fails he won't afford New Sera,' she said. 'We won't be compelled to divorce until they make it a free programme. That's –'

'That's leaving things to chance.' Pastor interrupted. 'My option –'

'He is a good man.' Amoit cut in. 'I won't hear of it.'

Pastor shrugged. 'So what might happen to his crop?'

'I don't know,' she said. 'It's failed before, but the projections look good for him now. I thought Congo was our best option, that's why –'

'The rock worm is another option.' Pastor interrupted her.

'What?'

'If we mix its eggs in the seed builder fluid, the agrobots will inject it into every cob. By morning they will have hatched and eaten up all the maize.'

'Rock worm?' A frown creased her forehead. It was a bio-engineered creature that looked like an earth worm. It turned whatever it ate into fertile soil. They used it to terraform barren, rocky lands, deserts and places that had perished due to severe pollution. Upon hatching it ate the nearest thing it found, be it rock, metal or maize cob. They sold it commercially in agro-shops, but one needed a special licence to buy it.

'Give me the garden's security code,' Pastor said. 'By morning, he will have a rock worm infestation.'

Amoit rode fast down the hill. The wind in her face thrilled her with a sense of danger, distracting her from the guilt of betraying her husband. She did not have protective padding on her knees and elbows, nor did she have a safety suit under the *gomesi*, but she was wearing a helmet, which was all traffic police looked out for. If she had an accident, she might be in hospital for a week. Would that throw suspicion off her after the rock worms ate up the garden? If the garden failed again he would be up to a million shillings in debt, and that wouldn't be the worst of it. He would lose his farm, which had been in his family for generations, and he would lose the bungalow. He would have to relocate to a free house in the city and live with the poorest of the poor.

With the population declining, free housing was not as horrible as it had been during Amoit's childhood. She grew up with her parents and three siblings in a two-bedroomed apartment, sharing a corridor with ten other families. The noise – the loud prayers in the middle of the night – had been the worst of it yet the absence of privacy had come a close second. There was less congestion now, so maybe she and Aceng would have enough privacy to consummate their love, but they would not have the luxury of eating good food. No more *matooke*, no more dairy products. They would feed on the *posho* and beans. Though the government provided free food, clothing, water and electricity to everyone, people still had to work. It would be unbiblical not to work. 'Only in heaven,' the Christian Council always said, 'shall we be free of labour.' Omongo would have to find a new job to pay off the debt. With the population decline, jobs were not hard to come by, but the economy was not in good shape, and he could only earn as much as she did, so he would have to work for the rest of his life to pay off the debt. He may never earn enough to afford New Sera. He would have to wait until it became a free service.

The bicycle reached the bottom of the hill. The road flattened, her speed dropped and she pedalled hard all the way back home. Sweat drenched her in spite of the *gomesi* fitted with an air con. Aceng opened the gate. She wanted to hug her right away, but waited until they were indoors.

'Are we going to Congo?' Aceng asked.

'There's a plan,' Amoit said, and told her about the rock worms.

They made love again, in the living room, but this time they took care to draw the curtains and close the doors.

When her husband returned later that evening, Amoit was watching a TV programme about a man who performed miracles during The Big Burn, saving thousands of lives. Omongo slumped into the sofa beside Amoit. When he wriggled his nose, she feared he had noticed the scent of sex.

'What's she cooking?' Omongo asked.

Amoit smiled in relief. '*Molokony*,' she said. He loved cow hooves.

'Hmmm,' he said, his face glowing. 'A perfect way to end a successful day. The agrobots say there were no errors during production. We expect to harvest up to ten tons.'

With a kilo going for twenty shillings, he would earn up to two hundred thousand from this harvest. It would not give him financial stability, but it would stop the debts from piling up. He would not have to borrow for the next round of gardening. In another five rounds, he would have cleared off his debts and he would have that financial stability that had eluded him since his father died.

'That's good news,' Amoit said. The agrobots had never given him such a good forecast.

He was horny that night and even though Amoit was spent from the two rounds with Aceng, she was anxious to wash away the guilt troubling her, so she did not turn him away. But she wasn't a good partner and she could feel his disappointment, so she started to give him a blow job. She had never given him one. Some Survivors of Gomorrah said they did it when they could not fully participate in making love to their partners. The choice came to her without her thinking about it. She found herself pushing his member into her mouth and sucking. He seemed to enjoy it for a few moments, but then he shoved her away.

'What are you doing?' he breathed angrily.

'Sorry,' she cried, just then remembering that a blow job was a sin, an immorality that made God very angry. 'Sorry, sorry, let's pray for forgiveness!'

She went down on her knees and broke into fervent prayer, blaming a demon that was trying to destroy her marriage. He joined her in the prayer. Thirty minutes later, the praying relented, and they chorused amen. They lay in bed for a long while, in silence. When he tried to make love to her again, she turned her back to him.

'The demon might tempt me again,' she said. 'Pastor has to pray for me. I need strength to resist temptation.'

The next day they went to church together. After the service, Pastor said to her: 'Your prayer request will be answered. This night watch out for a sign from God.' Then she knew that it had been done.

When she woke on Monday, he had already gone to the garden. She waited for him to call and tell her about the disaster, but he did not. She wanted to call Pastor, but they not could discuss such things over the phone. The police were always listening. At work she watched the phone all the time. It rang twice. She jumped each time, expecting Omongo to tell her about the disaster, but both calls were notices – one from the Mother's Union reminding her that she would host that week's Bible Study meeting scheduled for Tuesday. The other was from a man whose father had died without writing a will. He was calling to ask if Amoit could help his family sort out his estate. Each time the phone rang her heart beat faster. At five o'clock she hurried back home, expecting to find her husband there. He was not home yet. Shortly after six, while she was fixing supper with Aceng in the kitchen, they heard the bruka. She started to go up to the roof pad, but Aceng grabbed her arm.

'Stay here,' Aceng whispered. 'Act normal.'

They were making millet bread, so Amoit grabbed the mingling stick and began to knead the flour and the water. The heat from the solar stove warmed her face. With each second that passed, the flour became harder, making her use more effort to mix it for a smooth meal. Her hands trembled, but the effort reduced her panic. Aceng went out to clean the backyard, so that when Omongo entered the kitchen, Amoit was alone, fighting with *kaloo*. She became aware of his presence and turned around to him. There were tears on his face.

She turned off the stove and went over to him.

'What's the matter?' she said, hugging him. She was surprised at how calm she was.

'We lost it,' he said.

'What?' she said.

'The farm. It's all gone.'

He stepped away from her and sunk onto a stool, wiping his face with the back of his hand. She knelt in front of him, and he told her how he had found agrobots battling with a pest. He could not understand what was happening until he saw the worms eating up a robot, turning it into soil. He called the police, who threw a biobomb into the garden, releasing a gas that killed all the worms in a few seconds. By then, only a few strands of maize remained standing.

'It's because we sinned,' Omongo said.

'Sinned?' Amoit said.

'Saturday night,' Omongo said. 'You –'

'But we stopped!' Amoit interrupted. 'We prayed for forgiveness!'

'God is punishing me for your sin,' Omongo said.

He marched off before she could respond. She tried to follow him, but he turned quickly and pushed her. She flew into the kitchen and he vanished into the bedroom and locked himself in. When he emerged after more than an hour the sun had gone down. Amoit and Aceng were pretending to watch a TV programme about a famous choirmaster who was taught by angels. Amoit walked up to him. He allowed her to touch his arms, and he looked deep into her eyes. His lips trembled as though he wanted to say something but the words were stuck in his throat.

'Let's go to church and confess,' she said. 'God will show us a way.'

He turned away from her and ran up the stairs to the roof pad. She ran after him, but he did not look at her as he ignited the bruka and sped away. She stared at the darkness that had swallowed up his ornithopter, and she hated herself for what she had done to him.

She felt Aceng's hand on her shoulder, warm and damp with sweat. She let Aceng lead her back into the house. They kissed, but Amoit did not feel joy in that kiss. She pulled away. She sat heavily on the sofa, knowing she had ruined a man's life. She should not have tricked him into falling in love with her. Now he faced a lifetime in slavery, unable to own a bruka or his own house, maybe living off the government's Samaritan Programme for the Poor. He was a good man.

'Shall I make you a cup of hibiscus?' Aceng asked.

Amoit nodded. Hibiscus always helped her get out of a depressive mood. Some pastors had recently called for the banning of hibiscus and other herbs, saying they were toxic and contained drugs. Amoit wondered what draining a bottle of wine felt like. She knew about getting drunk because it was in the Bible, and some Survivors of Gomorrah had claimed to have got drunk after stealing wine meant for Holy Communion. She wondered if she would feel better if she got drunk. It would be easy to get a bottle. She would only have to go to Pastor.

They drank hibiscus and pretended to watch TV. Images flashed on the screen without her understanding what they stood for. Nearly two hours later, just as they prepared to go to bed, her phone rang. The caller tune, *What a Friend I have in Jesus*, was automatically assigned to a spouse. She answered the call, and at once heard a speedometer beeping in the background. He was in the bruka.

'Hello,' she said, her voice trembling.

'I love you,' Omongo said.

'I –' She could not say it. She swallowed hard. 'I'm sorry.'

'I left you a letter,' he said. She could hear beeping in the background, indicating that he was going over the speed limit. If he persisted, a traffic cop would go after him and he might spend a few days locked up.

'It's in my Bible,' he said.

'What are you talking about?' she asked.

'I love you, Amoit,' he said. He was crying. 'I've always loved you.'

'Omo!' she said, the fear showed in her voice. She had not called him Omo in a very long time. 'Omo!'

But the phone was dead. She called him back. He did not pick up. A few seconds later, they heard an explosion. It sounded like thunder. It rattled the window panes as though it were an earthquake. She instinctively felt that it had something to do with him. She ran out of the house, aware of Aceng behind her. From the yard they had a limited view of the city skyline, but they could see the reflection of the flames in the clouds, so they went up to the roof pad, where the view was better. The B-Gete building was on fire. After a few moments it exploded, lighting up the night with a display of fireworks.

'Omo,' she whispered, 'What have you done?'

'What letter was he talking about?' Aceng said.

Amoit ran into the house, into the bedroom, to his study table. The Bible lay beside a laptop. The screensaver was on: a slide show of video clips from their wedding. She shook the Bible and a brown piece of paper fell out. She picked it up, her fingers trembling as she read.

My love Amo, the letter begun. *I've loved you from the day I met you and I hope you loved me too.* The words blurred. She wiped her eyes with the back of her hand, and then she felt Aceng's warm bosom pressing into her back, her arms wrapping around her stomach. It felt like the hug her mother gave her the day her father passed away. She had been a little girl then, frightened of the demons that had made Baba sick.

If you find this letter before I call you, please do not call me. Do not say anything on the phone or on email. I'm sorry I've not been honest, but I know how devoted you are to Christ and I was afraid that you would tell the police about me. Pray for my soul. I lost faith the day I discovered the conspiracy of the Christian Council and B-Gete. We do not need genetically engineered crops. Natural seeds can do just as well in our gardens, but they want to control food production, so that they can take away our free will by feeding us hallucinogenic drugs. They do this to stop the rebellion. Yes, there is a rebellion but you won't hear of it in the news.

The letter explained how Omongo became a rebel. As his debts piled up, a man approached him and told him about the rebellion, showing him photos and videos of fighting and of when, two years ago, the army cordoned off Mbale City and used biobombs to wipe out every life form after rebels had gained control of it. That turned the rebels from a major threat into a small terrorist organisation. To stamp out all opposition, the Christian Council came up with a plan to feed the entire country hallucinogenic drugs. Seeing that the rebels might counter this by supplying seeds of their own, they came up with a scheme to enslave all farmers through debt. Omongo was not alone. No farmer had made any profit after switching to B-Gete seeds. Omongo did not believe this until he met other farmers, some of whom he knew, who all had enormous debts.

After the rock worm attack on his garden, Omongo was convinced it was a B-Gete sabotage. He asked the rebels if they had a bomb that could bring down the B-Gete building. He wanted revenge. It would be a suicide mission, but it would be a big blow to the Christian Council's mind-control programme. They would have no option but to allow natural seeds, and by the time they rebuild infrastructure and stock for their programme, maybe the rebels would have regained enough strength to continue the fight. The bomb would have to be packed into a bruka and he would have to ram his bruka into the B-Gete tower. It would flatten the tower. Though they might hide it from the news, the entire city would hear the explosion, and people would see that the tower missing from the skyline. Maybe that will get city folk to ask a lot of questions and maybe that will help people know about the rebellion from word of mouth – the way it had happened in Mbale City.

You will have a few hours as they sort through the rubble for clues. Before midnight they'll know I did it and they'll come for you. I hear they exterminate a rebel's entire family to discourage other rebels. I didn't want this to happen to you, but fanatics like you make this country hell. I hope you go to heaven.

Amoit stared at the paper for a long time. The only thing she felt was a disappointment that they had not been honest with each other. If he had known she was in love with Aceng, then he would have known she was not a devout Christian, and if only she had known he was involved with rebels, she would not have feared him to be a fanatic follower of the Christian Council. She let the letter slip out of her hand and it fell to the floor.

'We have to run,' Aceng said.

'But where can we go?' Amoit said.

'Pastor might know,' Aceng said.

Maybe, Amoit thought, there was a basement in the church. Maybe Pastor would allow them to hide until they figured a way out. They began to pack, thinking quickly about how to get to the church without being detected by the street cameras that were positioned everywhere, recording every move anyone in the village made.

Albus

JUSTIN DINGWALL

ARTIST STATEMENT

THE DISCOURSE ABOUT ALBINISM is generally taboo in South African. When discussed, it is usually viewed as negative or as a sought-after 'oddity' in fashion and art trends. The photographer and creator of the series, *Albus*, aims for an intimate perspective to foreground the myths surrounding albinism.

This series developed into an exploration of the aesthetics of albinism in contrast to the idealised perceptions of beauty. It began as an interest to capture something not conventionally perceived as 'beauty'. The artist began this project with the ethereal portraits of Thando Hopa, a legal prosecutor who is using her visibility to address the negative perceptions surrounding albinism. The artist's inspiring new work features Sanele Xaba, a young model with albinism, and uses specific elements to highlight the symbolic meaning behind each work.

The artist's intention is for the images to become a celebration of beauty in difference. 'They are not about race or fashion, but about perception and what we subjectively perceive as beautiful. I wanted to create a series of images that resonate with humanity and make people question what is beautiful.'

The artist's interest lies in the unique and the different. 'To me, diversity is what makes humanity interesting and beautiful.' The artist has foregrounded certain elements in his work. These symbols have inspired his perceptions as an artist, and are significant in his intention to affect viewers' perspectives.

The symbols of light and dark are a reflection of his medium. The artist uses the characteristic nature of photography to capture a unique frame of reference. The artist paints with light in such a way as to represent the revealing of the unseen. Light represents truth, and it is contrasted against the element of darkness to emphasise the unenlightened state of mind of previous misconceptions.

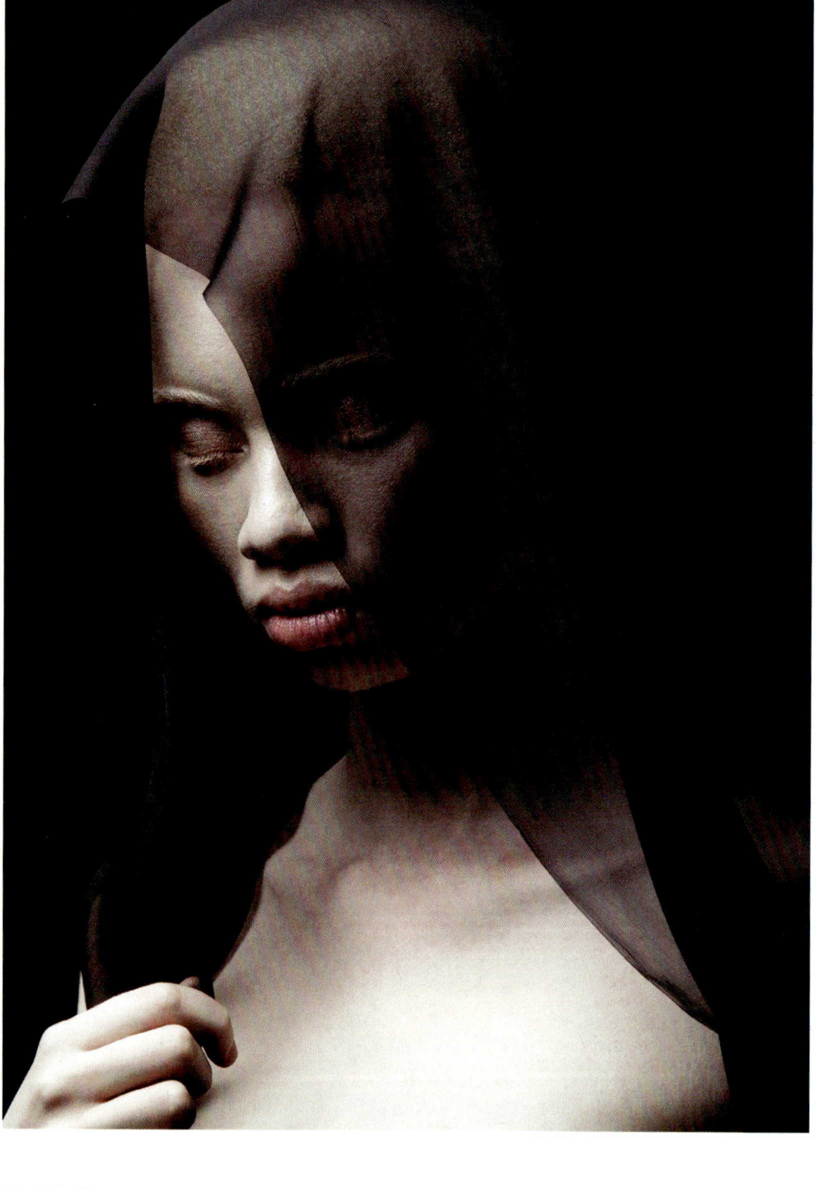

Black Veil

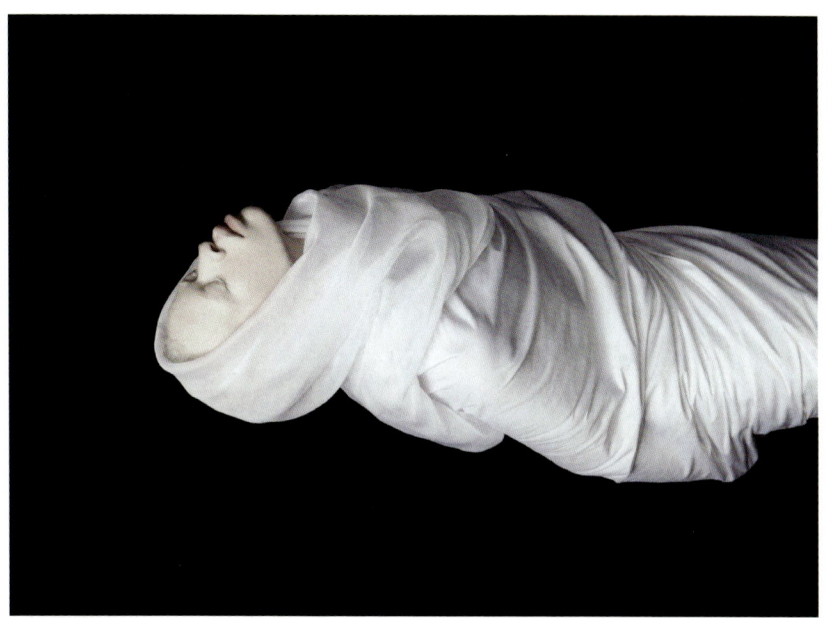

TOP: Embrace
BOTTOM: Ubuntu

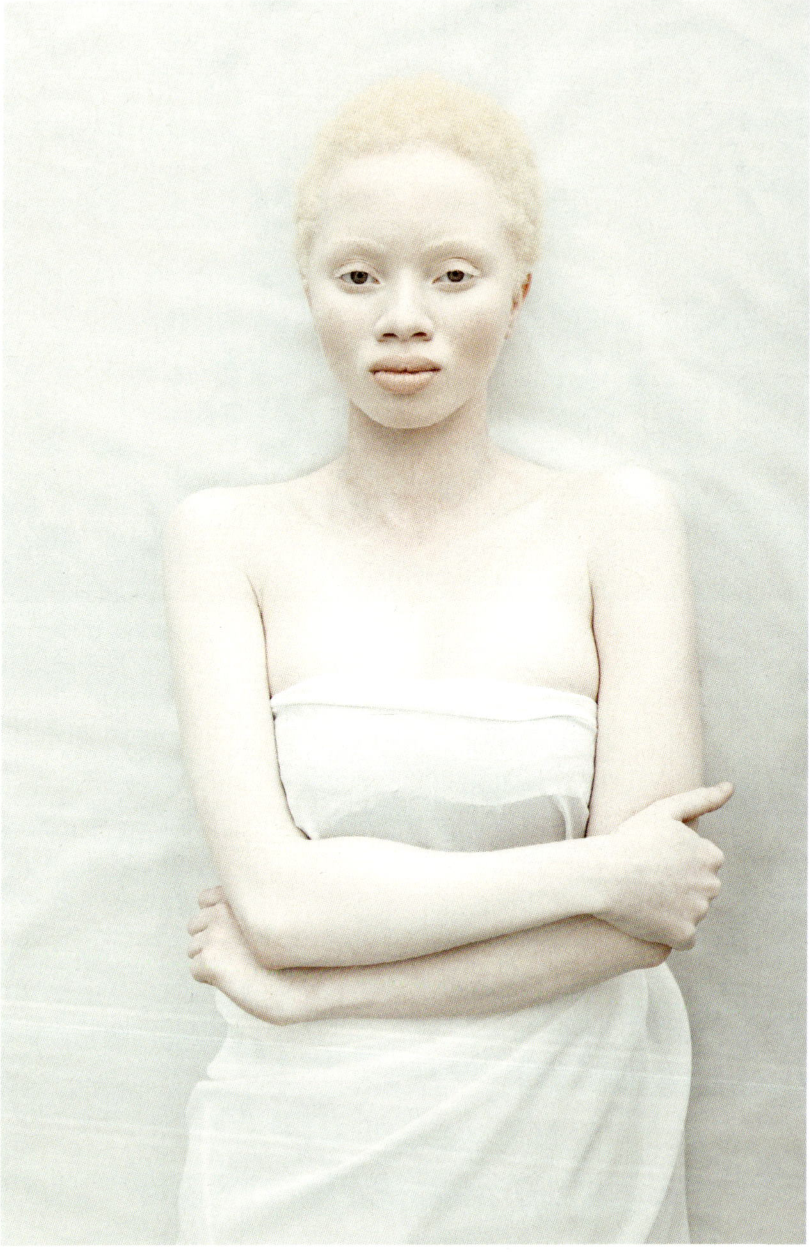

Vulnerable Eyes Open

Vulnerable Eyes Closed

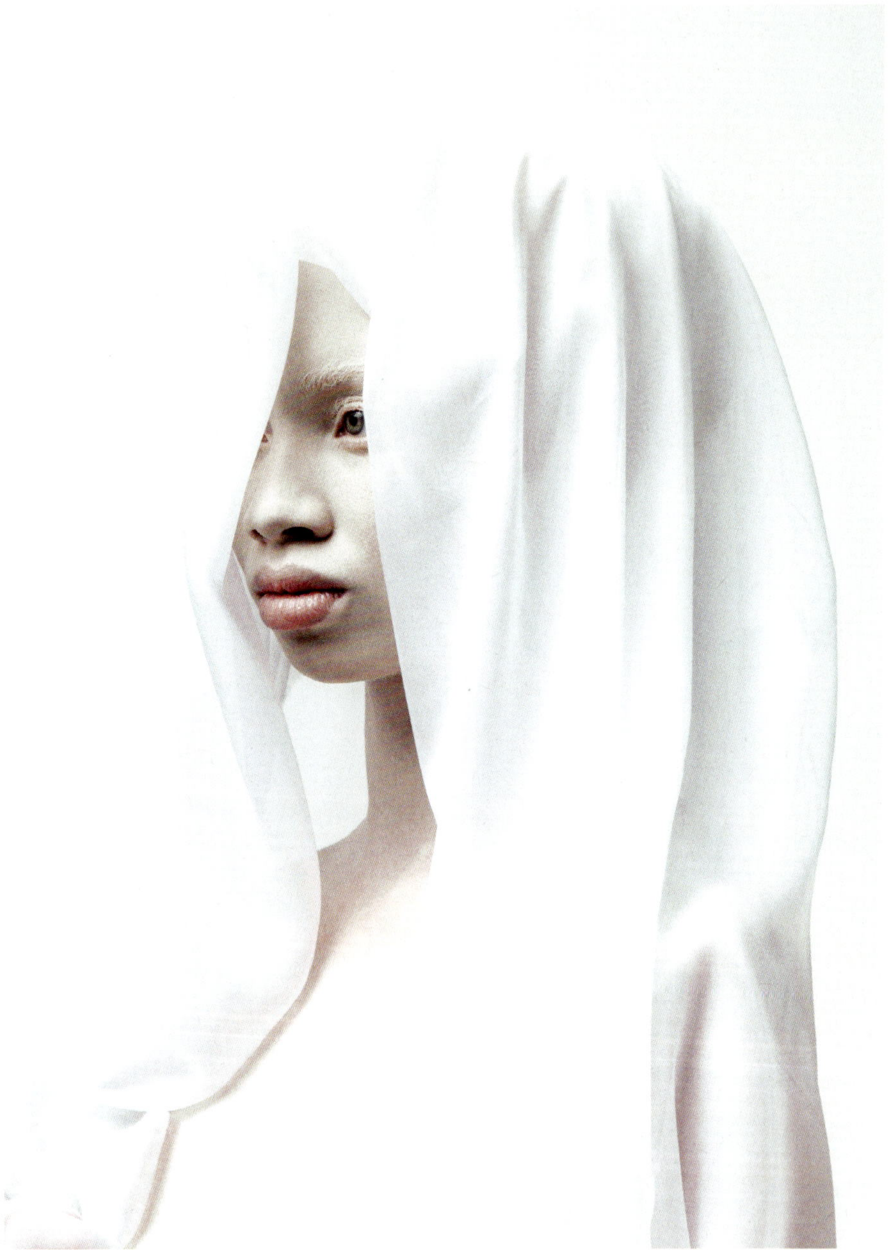

White Veil

IN WITH THE NEW

We, as a society, are uncomfortable to acknowledge the prevalence of albinism in our country. There are many misconceptions that attach a severe social stigma to people with albinism, including witchcraft and not fitting in with society's norms.

Albinism is a congenital disorder resulting in the production of little to no pigmentation in the skin, hair and eyes. This is what creates the physical difference in outward appearance that people with albinism are ostracised for.

The artist has made a conscious effort to portray an intimate perspective in his imagery to foreground the myths surrounding albinism.

Water is a major element in the image 'In with the new'. Imagery of water has featured in many of the world's myths and legends. It is a transparent liquid that is the major component of all living things.

Water is often used as a symbol of change in literature and often signifies a turning point in a story. The artist aims for this image to be a turning point in society's 'story', for people to view albinism differently.

Water reflects – and this is what invites people to engage in the act of refection. This is portrayed in the myth of Narcissus, which suggests the hypnotic power a reflection holds. Water was the first surface that served as a mirror for humankind. The artist wants the viewer to be drawn into the image as if it were a mirror and to make people take a closer look at themselves, to question their own judgements about others. The reflection of Sanele in the image is aimed to represent the mirror image of the viewer, so that they see themselves in the image – and not an 'other'.

Water is also a symbol for cleansing. It is believed that people are purified through the process of washing, which the artist hopes will result in the viewer reflecting on their own beliefs and washing away their previous misconceptions.

The artist has also chosen to feature the symbolism of the colour white, as it depicts connotations to albinism.

In colour psychology, white depicts new beginnings. The image of 'wiping the slate clean', leaving us with a blank white canvas, represents a new outlook on previous ideas and misconceptions. While white isn't a colour that stimulates the senses, it clears the mind for creation.

In the colour spectrum, white contains an equal amount of all the colours, representing both positive and negative elements of each shade. Its most important feature – in the eyes of the artist – is equality. This suggests impartiality and neutrality, which leads to the neutral perspective the artist hopes to achieve. White, like water, is reflective, suggesting growth and self-reflection. The colour white is also like water in the way that cleansing and emptying the pallet clears the viewer's thoughts for new possibilities.

'In with the new' comes from the English saying 'out with the old'. This is to represent the 'clean slate', the fresh perspective and the new perceptions that the artist hopes the viewer will achieve. Out with our old preconceived ideas and in with change and a new perspective.

REBIRTH

Images of serpents have featured in many of the world's myths and legends. The artist has chosen to portray snakes as a major element in the image 'Rebirth'.

In the process of growth, snakes often shed their skins to reveal a new skin underneath. For this reason snakes have become symbols of rebirth, transformation, immortality and healing.

By using the snake, the artist aims to influence the viewer's vision to be reborn, allowing them to view albinism in a new light – as something unique and beautiful.

People tend to fear what they do not understand. The artist hopes to affect people's views, to persuade them to confront their misconceptions, inner fears and personal judgements. The artist hopes to allow viewers to observe albinism not as a negative issue, but as a part of a person as a whole.

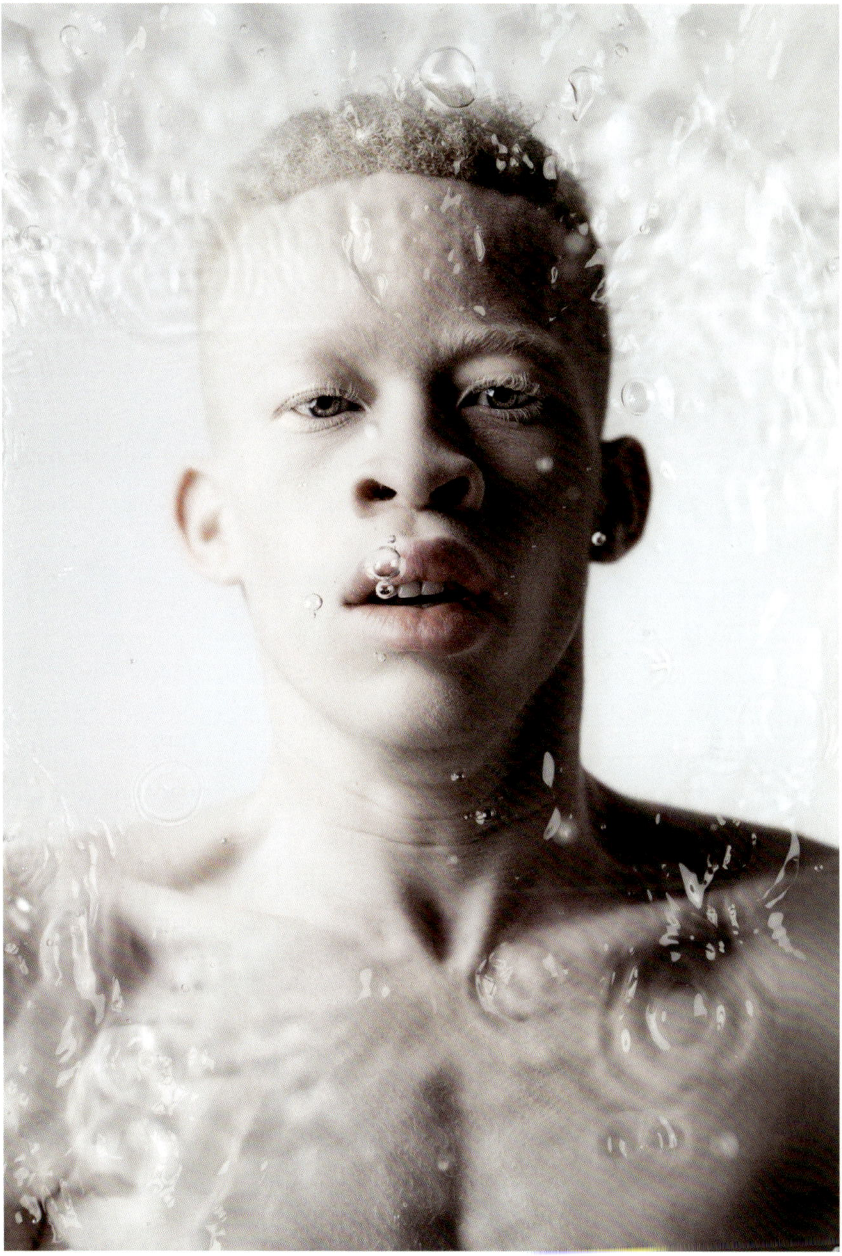

In With the New

The snake also symbolises healing in some literary traditions. They are viewed to be able to rejuvenate and are believed to have eternal qualities. In medical discourse the Rod of Asclepius, the image of a snake wrapped around a rod, is a symbol associated with medicine and healthcare.

Guardianship is another symbol that snakes represent in certain cultures. In 'Rebirth', the python is draped across Sanele's shoulders and head, staring out into the darkness with a fixed gaze, while Sanele's yes are closed in a meditative state. The snake symbolises protection, keeping watch while allowing Sanele to just be.

Sanele represents the strength of uniqueness; he portrays that each person is an individual who has something to contribute to the greater whole of humanity.

In this image the artist asked Sanele to face one of his major fears: slithering reptiles. This fear is one that is common among some African cultures.

Snakes have long been associated with evil as well as good, representing death and life, destruction and creation.

The image is divided into two halves: light and darkness. This is to symbolise past and present. The darkness represents the unenlightened state of mind of previous misconceptions. The more knowledge people have, the better equipped they are to understand someone else. The light symbolises knowledge, which enlightens.

Sanele is foregrounded in light. Light represents truth because light reveals the unseen. People trust their sight more than any of their other senses. People are so confident in the power of sight to reveal the truth that they often use expressions such as 'seeing is believing' or 'shedding light on the matter'.

This image is intended to elevate and bring albinism to light. The artist wanted to create a portrait in the style of the classical Dutch painters, which would also have the same sculptural quality of a Grecian bust. The artist doesn't view differences in humanity as abject; in his view diversity is what makes humanity interesting and beautiful.

Rebirth

Resurrection[1]

TANIA HABERLAND

The sea is a grave of shells.

Each one a stroked pearl
of silent wisdom entombed.
Each one a slick clitoris housed –

stone walls are licked open,
a water phoenix rises
from pulverised shell,

iridescent powder lurches forward
from cold into the warm
sun breath on the sea.

Everything shines.

---

1 '...the contradictions of the shell, which at times is so rough outside and so soft, so pearly, in its intimacy. How is it possible to obtain this polish by means of friction with a creature that is so soft and flabby? And doesn't the finger that dreams as it strokes, the intimate mother-of-pearl surface surpass our human, all too human, dreams?' – Gaston Bachelard, *The Poetics of Space,* p.115

For men who care

AMATESIRO DORE

I ADEY

'How much are you going to pay me?' The guy was talking to me but I couldn't believe this was happening.

It was five a.m. – three hours after having sex – and he was drinking on my bed. I was dressed and ready to drop him off, but he decided to scandalise our sexual encounter.

'How much do you want?'

'How much do you think my ass is worth?'

'I can afford ten thousand now. I will have to use a cash machine to get more.'

He smashed the glass and red wine splattered on my wall. I collapsed on my knees and started to beg. This changed the game.

'I will give you anything. Just don't make a noise.'

'The whole of Ikoyi will gather if I don't get my money now!'

My best friend and his fiancée were sleeping in the opposite room, my father was in his wing across the courtyard and our house helps would start their Saturday morning cleaning before six. I couldn't explain returning home, from a nightclub, with a guy. I couldn't even remember his name.

'You think you can just fuck me scatter for free?' The guy clapped his hands and laughed while I remained on my knees. I started to cry.

His voice threatened to make me fatherless and without a friend in the world. It had never been more obvious to me that I couldn't trust anyone with the truth about myself. I swore to kill him for robbing me of the lies that allowed me to sleep and wake up every day.

'You sabi fuck man, but you nor wan pay. Today breeze don blow and everybody go see your yansh.'

He didn't speak pidgin when I met him at the VIP. It was the year of the Ace of Spades and my table had plenty. It was one of those nights when friends from abroad, fellow gentlemen of the bar and familiar residents of the island somehow appeared at the same club, at the same period, to thank God for Friday. He was a fresh, young guy, smiling like the sun on the blinking cold dance floor. His tattoos flashed from sleeveless gymed arms and our eyes mated – several times – in a club filled with women. I fancied him because there was nothing effeminate about him. He was just a random well-dressed dude, chilling in the club without the company of babes or guys.

'Hey! Come chill with us,' I said and passed him a bottle to refill his glass.

I made him laugh, kept his glass refilled and ensured he remained within a touch away. What did we talk about? The yarns of tipsy men: women, sex and pussy.

'Are you getting hard?' I swept my palm over his regions.

'I've not had pussy in a long time,' he laughed into my eyes.

'What have you been having?' I asked and he laughed on my shoulder.

At that hour when drinking buddies switched clubs or returned home with a date or girlfriend, I left cash for a chunk of the bill and sneaked out with him. He lived on the mainland and didn't mind sleeping in Ikoyi that night. The other option was to hop from club to club until five a.m. when it would be safe to cross the Third Mainland Bridge.

'You can crash at my place if you promise not to rape me,' I said as we laughed all the way to my car.

'I promise to moan softly and no one will hear me scream when I come,' he said. I thanked God for meeting him.

My best friend was visiting from Port Harcourt to spend a weekend with his Lagos-based fiancée. I'd known Tonye since secondary school. We attended different universities, but our mothers presided over different divisions of the Court of Appeal. His fiancée's car was in my car park when I drove in with my Conquest. I wondered if they could hear the early morning drama unfolding in my room.

'Don't try anything funny – I kept the condoms you used to burst my yansh,' the guy said and brought out a wad of tissues from his pocket.

He made me sign an undertaking to pay him two hundred thousand naira 'for fucking' him. I decided not to leave him alive because of the risk of exposure.

'Let's go to the ATM,' I said. He crept out of my room with glee in his eyes.

Within the wealth and prestige of Ikoyi, there were bad roads without streetlights and isolated avenues avoided by pedestrians at night. I found an ideal spot and smashed a bottle on his head. He flew out of my car and I ran after him. I caught up with his bleeding head and we struggled for the evidence in his pocket. After many blows and unanswered cries for help, he threw the tissue in one direction and ran opposite. I found the condoms, buried them and drove after him. But he hid from me, so I didn't find him after driving up and down the street. As dawn and joggers appeared, my rage fizzled out and I returned home.

The worst part was that I couldn't tell anyone. I couldn't share my shame and receive consolation for my pain. I'd dug my grave deep inside the closet and no one could hear me cry.

II EMEKA

After many years you saw him again, but there was age in his eyes, stress on his smile and the experience of a thousand lives rested on his *agbada*. He was no longer the fine boy you once met. A refined man was wearing his skin and something had humbled his heart.

'Hello, it's me!' Adey said. His baritone voice reminded you of his naked skills.

You hugged him. His musk of wealth, his breath like wine and his heavyweight chest intoxicated your soul.

'Where have you been?' He asked as he led you to one of the many empty tables at the ritzy restaurant in Ikoyi. A waiter appeared to take your order, as though it was a pre-arranged date, and not a scene of serendipity in action. You wanted to run away when you remembered the unanswered phone calls, ignored messages and social-media blocking after he seduced your soul, banged your brains out and flushed away your existence with his condoms. Your spirit said you should leave, but your body smiled at every word that came out of his sweet mouth that had once churned your ass into butter.

'What are you doing here?' he asked. You told him about the South-East Asian rice that made you drive from Apapa to Ikoyi that Saturday afternoon.

'No wonder you're now carrying extra shock absorbers,' he said, and you became conscious of the roundness of your belly, your flabby arms and cushy behind.

Your days at the gym had passed, but the muscles of your bank accounts could crush his trust fund and all the proceeds from his decade-long legal career. You deflected his lascivious scrutiny of your fleshly insecurities with questions about his life. He answered like an old friend, volunteering details of his private life, and the realisation gouged out your eyes: Adey was out and balling in Nigeria.

'Yeah, all my friends know, including my colleagues at work. My sexuality is stale news.'

Of course he could get away with it, you thought – his mother was on the bench of the supreme court and his father served three different commander-in-chiefs of the armed forces. The law was for the poor and unconnected, a tool for blackmail and police extortion. It was to remind people like you of their place beneath society, irrespective of wealth and personal achievements.

'I was friends with this guy at church,' Adey said, feeding your courage. 'He was from one of those families who drove all the way from the mainland to attend church in Ikoyi. We went to school at about the same time, but he attended a state university in the east. When this guy was in school, I would send him pocket money. I gave him the laptop he used to write his final year thesis. I gave him money to travel up north for National Youth Service Corps. Even when he was getting married, I went with my friends to his wedding in Enugu. Suddenly, after this guy married a senator's daughter, he changed it for me. It was much later that I heard he had been saying shit about me, how I never had a girlfriend, blah, blah, blah.'

'Then I noticed he was acting weird, like he didn't invite me to his child's birthday and other celebrations but invited my friends and other people he met through me. Finally, I confronted him and the son of a bitch asked, "Are we really friends?" I was, like, "What do you mean by that? After almost fifteen years of enjoying my money, you are asking if we're really friends, you gold-digging bitch!"

'I didn't even like him that way and I never made a pass at him. The ugly motherfucker wasn't my type. He was just a friend from an under-privileged family. When he went about trying to make my childhood friends cut me off, it boomeranged on him. We cut off the bitch but he changed my mind set. That experience made me admit my sexuality to my close friends, so I could get rid of them if I needed to, but I was surprised by their reactions.'

'My best friend said he had known since puberty, but he never confronted me because he never gave a fuck about it. After that I just became myself.'

And you fell in love with the pain in his eyes, the vulnerability of his heart and the pride puffing up his chest. As he spoke, his words gathered the detritus of your heart and like Humpty Dumpty you were put together again.

'But that guy made me hate weddings and I became suspicious of my straight friends. I cut off everyone like him, anyone who was financially dependent on me and those who needed my friendship to survive. I refuse to pay for my sexuality, to bribe people for friendship or to permit anyone to tolerate me because of my parents or what I have.'

You asked if he was wearing a wedding *aso-ebi* and he confirmed your guess. You asked why he wasn't at the wedding and he said he left the reception when he realised the newlyweds wouldn't attend his wedding if he invited them. Why, you asked.

'Because I want to get married to a guy, get divorced if it doesn't work out and remarry like every other fucking person. I hope to meet a Nigerian guy and have a lavish Nigerian society wedding with my friends and family in attendance.'

Those were the words that changed your life. You never knew a man could care for another. You hadn't known that a Nigerian man could love at the risk of death, that any African man could pledge his life to another man. He wasn't perfect and he wasn't proposing, but you were willing to try to fall in love and have your heart broken, like every other human being. If Adey could love himself, and be himself, there was hope for you and for men who care in Nigeria.

III ALIYU

After many wars, violence eventually fizzled out in the Middle East and the faithful of northern Nigeria disavowed fighting for God. In the cosmopolitan city of Kano, the Muslims remained Muslims and the Christians remained Christians, but Aliyu Danladi became Aisha Danladi and no one killed her for substituting the male appendage between her legs.

Everyone was curious about the three wives Aliyu had married during his service in the Nigerian Army. News bloggers reported that the retired chief of Army Intelligence had divorced the mothers of his children within one month, like a man converting to Christianity. He gave them gifts of cash and property, like a polygamous man with a few months to live. And he visited the Kano General Hospital, like someone undergoing cancer treatment and counselling. After a few years of evaluations, therapies and surgeries, the sixty-five-year-old decorated general became Aisha Danladi on Facebook and her profile picture showcased the best makeup and cosmetic surgeries anyone could buy.

On the Friday after her Facebook profile update, she was photographed at the Central Mosque where fellow Muslims prayed with her and reserved judgement for heaven. Aisha retained the distrust Aliyu had had of the media and so she refused to grant any interviews. She did, however, post a few tweets:

I have lived for my family, society and country.

After retiring from public service, I have decided to live my life for myself.

Following a few days of headline news, the metamorphosis of General Danladi faded from media coverage. The novelty of her high-profile transition became a mere reminder of old-school bigotry and twentieth-century ignorance.

In the privacy of her bedroom, Aisha mourned the death of Aliyu and a life once lived. He had been a good man who loved women beyond what was superficial: their hair, their voices, their bodies. He had been a good son who obeyed his parents and allowed them to choose his faith, his career and his first wife. He had been a good citizen who had served his community and country. He had evolved and learned to listen, understand, read and empathise. And at the age of sixty he realised he didn't just love women, he was one and he needed to live as one.

Aliyu's wives had never been a career subterfuge to camouflage his sexuality. He lived at the bottom of the pyramid of needs: there were bills to pay, children to feed and a country rode on his back into political stability. There was never enough time to focus on his identity before his children left home, before his parents slept and died, before his wives flourished in their careers and before he retired from military service. That was when the pursuit of life diminished and the pursuit of happiness overtook his mind. It wasn't his intention to break up his family and make them tabloid fodder; he just wanted personal happiness after supplying it to others for sixty years.

His first wife was the first person to hear about his decision to live happily ever after. As his best friend and companion of forty years, she wondered if he cheated on her and his other wives with other men.

'I have never been with a man,' Aliyu said and he swore on the Holy Name.

'But you like men?' she fumed.

'I haven't considered them and I honestly don't know.'

She believed him because he had that look in his eyes. The one he had when he confessed his attraction for the beautiful woman who became his second wife. The look of helplessness over what he could never change, even if he tried. She didn't speak to him for many months until she couldn't bear to ignore the face that broke her heart.

'You will wait,' she said. 'You must wait until we're divorced, and every one of us must have found suitable partners before you change.'

And Aliyu waited for five years for his ex-wives to settle into new marriages, because he was a man who cared.

Intertwined odyssey

JULIA HANGO

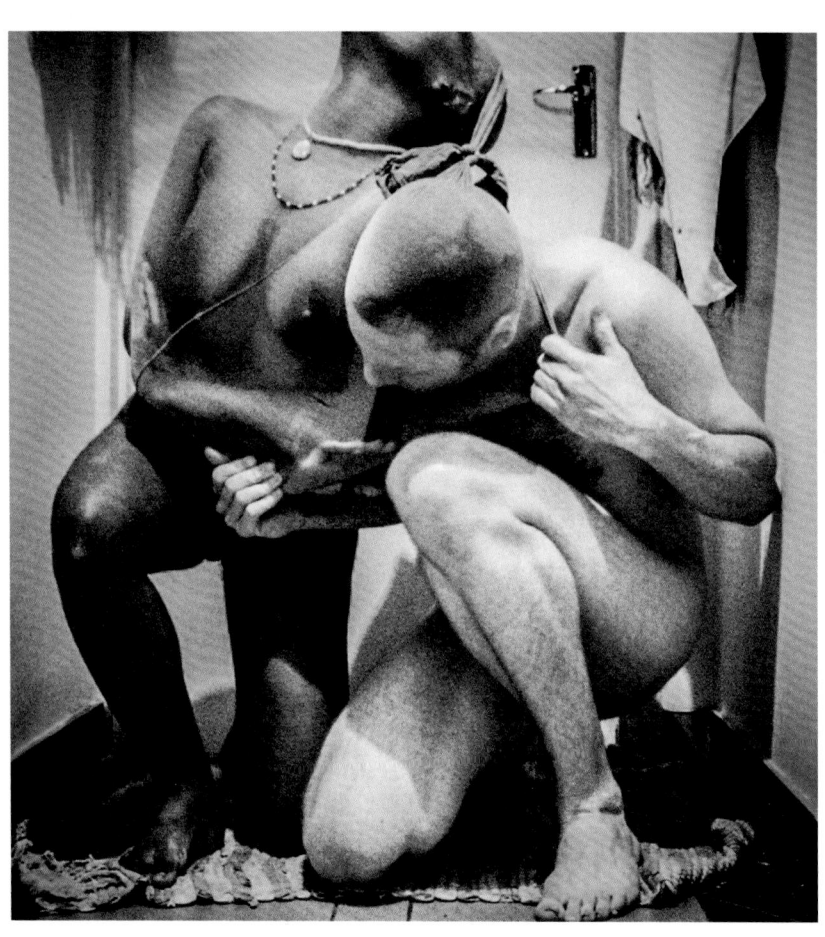

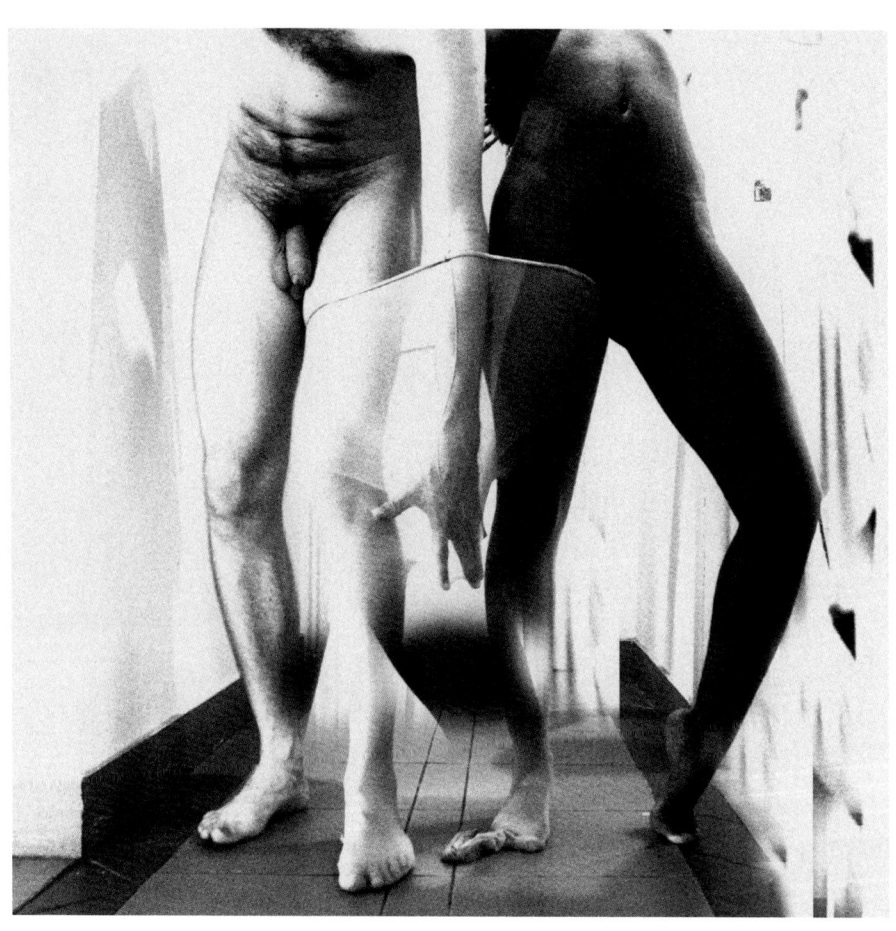

You sing of a longing

OTOSIRIEZE OBI-YOUNG

Your life is a blooming tulip:
white and un-whittled, wet and un-warm.
In its peopled loneliness, you are discovering desire,
unearthing the live wire that will tie you to things you will never have.
You are opening a love book of longings.

1.

THE MANGOES START TURNING REDDISH and yellowish that April when he begins coming to Christ the King Cathedral field. You often see him jogging in his green-and-white Super Eagles jersey and sparkling red boots, or stretching himself on the dark brown sand in the pitch, or in the canteen buying snacks and drinks, or sitting in his black Jeep that's under the mango tree, a stone's throw from the field. It is four months into 2000, and all talk about the world failing to end in 1999 has died; the world has moved on very quickly. You're still nine, still carrying footballs to CKC to play four-against-four with your friends. On TV, Nigeria has just lost on penalties to Cameroon in the Africa Cup of Nations final. On the streets, the Bakassi Boys are intensifying their arrests. They're publicly butchering robbers in major junctions – robbers and people suspected of being robbers. They're dousing their bodies with petrol, setting them ablaze in the centre of cheering crowds. They're throwing their burnt-black bodies into Borrow Pit along the expressway. Sometimes, though, when it is the crowd that has burnt the robbers, the bodies will be left there in the centre of traffic, as a warning to eyes, as an impediment to noses.

That April, a few days after you begin seeing him, your coach introduces him to the team. He is average in height, not very fair, not very muscled, but with a bushy beard. He says he used to lecture in Nsukka, but this is what the love of football has turned him into: a coach. With a whistle between his pink lips, he dishes out instructions in English, sharing balls, having each of you bounce it up to a hundred times, saying, 'Terrific, terrific,' while clapping softly. Later he asks you all, one by one, to name one other thing you are talented in, anything you want to be besides a footballer. When it gets to your turn, you say: 'Musician.'

'Musician,' he repeats, nodding and smiling. 'So you want to be the next Fela?'

There's something about his presence, his standing there, about the refusal of his hands to stay still even as they clasp that bottle of water. There's something about the guttural bass of his voice, his grin that is a brown sketch of teeth, his eyes that point at you with something you haven't seen before, his sweet smell of sweat and body spray. There's something that prises you open, threatens to rearrange everything inside your brain. You feel a sudden need to close up, to seal yourself, to take back your words, to say that you actually want to be a doctor or lawyer or engineer like the others, so that his eyes that look like they want to fall back into their sockets will leave you. You want to get up and walk away from there and get as far away as you can.

Many years later, when you'll drop football and begin stalking radio DJs to give them CDs of your songs, when you'll begin feeling a revolving emptiness, a gratitude for the invaluable moments when you felt a small lucid sanity, you'll return daily to this evening to seek validation from the calm eyes of a stranger. But now he is smiling as he asks everyone's name again, as he says once more: 'My own name is Dr Uzodinma. You can call me Coach.' And you watch the words leave his lips, watch them float in the air, swing slowly downwards like leaves, and you stare at his beard and see beads of water dripping off it. Later, when you get home, you open the notebook where you paste images of bare-bodied men cut out from newspapers – Zinedine Zidane, Mohammed Ali, Fela Kuti – and wonder how he would look in your book.

December 2007 and you are nineteen. You have failed twice to gain admission to Nsukka, and have styled your hair into a Mohawk because you are an aspiring artist, because the only males not harassed by the soldiers for their hair are footballers and aspiring artists. It is now, seven years later, that you see him again, and in the weeks that follow, you will realise how much of the world is beyond your grasp.

Something keeps you distracted that evening and you keep watching the white Jeep. When the driver alights in an all-blue long-sleeved Chelsea top and trousers, you watch him too. After more than thirty minutes of watching him jog the length of the pitch, after he has sat on the sand and has begun stretching, you start to walk towards him. 'Where are you going, Zukora?' someone shouts. *'Kee ebe I na-aga?* It's our set.'

That question will stick in your mind. *Where are you going?* A constant reminder that there are things you will never fully know about yourself.

'Good evening, sir,' you say, lowering your head. And suddenly, now that you are close, you become unsure, a part of you pricking up, insisting it is not him.

'Good evening,' he says, distractedly. He looks up.

You tell him you are one of the boys he once coached there seven years ago.

At first, he looks blank. Then his face loosens into a smile. 'Ah, I remember now. *Kee ka I mekwaranu?*' He is taking you in, shaking his head in mild amazement. 'You're a big boy now.'

'I'm fine, sir. I hope everything is fine with you,' you say, smiling.

'Yes, yes,' he says. For a second his eyes seem to focus on something beside you, and then he looks up, sipping from his bottle of water. 'Yes. Sit with me.'

You sit on the sand, warm and pale brown, punctuated here and there by yellowed tufts of withering grass. If this were the rainy season, the grass would be shiny green and wet, intensely itchy on bare skin. He leans backwards, his body supported by his hands, his hairy legs pulled up so that, from the border of his shorts, the white underwear he is wearing shows. It hits you again: the smell of the same body spray after so many years suddenly makes you want to urinate.

Near the goalpost, three children are in a circle, chanting Ruff Coin's *Nwa Aba*: '*Abum Nwa Aba, Aba, Aba ooo, Aba!*' Their voices so brittle, so fierce in their declaration that each of them is a *Nwa Aba*, a child of Aba in blood and character.

'My name is Zukora, sir,' you offer.

He nods. 'Zukora.'

You chat for some time, football matters: about the Golden Eaglets' U-17 World Cup victory days ago; his support for Chelsea because of Didier Drogba – even though Drogba scored and knocked out Nigeria in the Nations Cup semi-finals the previous year – and Michael Essien and Mikel Obi; your support for Barcelona because of Samuel Eto'o and Ronaldinho; who among Kaka, Messi and Cristiano Ronaldo deserves to win the 2007 FIFA World Player of the Year. It is growing dark when he says, 'Where do you live?'

'Ngwa Road.'

'That's close to my hotel.'

You are looking at him. He gets up, beats the sand off his buttocks. 'Come,' he says, walking towards his Jeep.

Around girls you have an idea of what to be, when to be it, what to do and how to do it. Around boys you are often lost, stilted, wilting. Every touch is awkward, and you feel as though something in you has been ripped off its hinges. You feel a riveting violation of confidence, an entrenchment of confusion.

You wake up naked under a blanket in his hotel room. It is morning. You look at him in his boxers, bare-bodied and with a white towel around his neck, and you feel a clenching in your chest, a fear. You murmur, 'Good morning, sir,' and he turns.

He catches the shivering in your eyes. He stares at you. He sits down on the bed. 'You were –' his hands move to and fro, in demonstration. 'You were touching me in the night. I thought you wanted me to …' His eyes are clear black suns in white skies.

How could I have wanted this? you want to scream at him. *How could I not have?* you scream at yourself.

You remember the bar and drinking with him. You remember him joking that the drink was too strong for your head. You remember downing one more shot to show him. You remember worrying that maybe you weren't experienced enough to know how to handle the shiny attention of a man old enough to be your father.

He begins apologising, embarrassed. His head drops and a clutter of 'sorries' spill across the room. His apology becomes desperate. 'I didn't know,' he is saying.

Finally you say, 'I remember.'

Then you get up, dress and open the door, and he says, 'Zukora.'

You stop at the door. 'Thank you,' he says. Still with your back to him, you nod quickly, not knowing what else to do.

Later on the phone, after thanking him and after he has said, 'We'll talk later,' you quickly say, 'Wait,' and he says, 'What?'

'I love you,' you say.

Silence follows.

Silence continues.

'You don't know the meaning of what you're saying,' he says finally. And hangs up.

And calls again.

'You don't even know me very well.'

But there are things that don't always ask for permission before happening. You know you are changing – something is making you happier, making you sadder. You are at that point in your life when everything suddenly has meaning, but neither too much nor too little – only enough meaning for you to take life as it comes, as it tries to take you apart, tries to work at the little compartments you have boxed your life into.

To be in love is to walk along Ngwa Road filled with taxis and buses and lorries, and hear the trilling of birds in and among all that horning and honking. It is to hear the chirping of invisible crickets near rubbish-filled gutters, a glorious a cappella soaring above the hurled shouts of drivers and motorcyclists. It is to pass by the towering refuse heap in the middle of Asa Road and perceive the absolute smell of nothing in the torn air. To be in love is to sit at home and let your eyes follow scurrying rats, your ears hear whining mosquitoes. It is to let cockroaches escape the soles of your stomping feet and to not have it occur to you to wish them ill. To be in love is to witness, on a June evening on Ogbor Hill, burnished-white clouds, a setting copper sun and an azure sky paint themselves into a river, skyscraping tree foliage and marshes on its aerial banks. It is to walk in the windy rain using your umbrella as a walking stick, enjoying a wholesome splattering.

To be in love is to feel a lightness of being, in being. It is to feel a god of little things, a granter of miracles in the most meaningless of moments, rising in your belly. It is to have a You-shaped hole in the universe, to imagine that all of creation is in sync with your mind. It is to see a glow in the distant eyes of Ahia Ohuru market traders, to feel warmth in the bus conductor's rudeness. To be in love is to imagine defiantly – to believe defiantly – that the object of your hunger will always lie in your sight. To love is to have the luxury of options and to choose to be unshackled.

But to be in love is to possibly also be a stray child at a busy road junction. You might have a deep cleft in you, a gnawing on the edges of your mind that scatters your head, unspools fear in your heart, and sets loose confusion that makes you imagine you're quietly going mad.

He doesn't talk about it when you next see him. Instead, he talks about school while you burn away. He cradles your head against his chest and tells you about his time as a lecturer in Nsukka. He asks why you don't want to sit for another admissions exam and tells you that you can combine your music pursuits with school.

You can't, you say quietly. 'My father's burial took away everything we had. My sister's illness, too. I can't be going to school when there are problems at home. It'll be like throwing away money.'

'School can never be like throwing away money.'

'In my case right now, it would be. I can't imagine spending four years incurring all those costs and then spending a few more years carrying files up and down, looking for a job I will never get. If I must gamble, then I will gamble on something I believe in.'

Each evening it is more or less the same thing, the same talk indulged because he initiates it, as if saying the same things absolve him from saying those other things. The two of you go to and fro, to and fro, until you fall silent. And then he picks up your hand in a warm clasp and helps it to snake down his torso. You grasp his erection and he chuckles. You bend and lick it and he moans, your fingers move all over him until he turns you over and kisses your back all the way down your backbone. Sometimes he doesn't go all the way, sometimes at this point he gets up and goes into the bathroom and you lie there, exposed, feeling ripped off, turbulence brewing beneath your skin. Sometimes you sob in sharp breaths and when he comes out, he cradles you to his body, touches your penis and asks, 'You didn't release?'

Each night, as you walk home, you try hard to not hear his voice in the shouts of drivers, to not see his oblong face in a patch on the tar, to not feel his fingers against your skin in the cold.

One evening, rising naked from the bed, he asks, 'Would you like to go out?'

He is facing the wardrobe with his back to you and you watch the symmetry of his muscled arms, the bony plunge of his lower back, the feminine elegance of his toes. He has shown you desire, has guided you to discover the small flames it breathes, and every single time you lay eyes on him you feel a small trembling in your veins, the rush of blood still unsatisfied.

You are behind him on his motorcycle, your body pressed against his, your hands around his waist as he speeds down Ngwa Road and up Obohia Road. You are heading down potholed Port Harcourt Road when he shouts, 'Were you serious when you said you loved me?'

'Yes.' The word pushes out before you recover from his casualness.

'Well, I love you, too!'

You're surprised; you nod.

'Did you hear me?'

'Yes, sir!'

That night, when you get home, you remove your clothes and stand naked before your mirror, trying to see yourself through his eyes. Afterwards, you touch yourself and cry in joy and fear.

But a week later, after he says he will call but doesn't, you arrive at his room. You knock and knock and knock until a fat man in a white towel opens the door with a frown. 'Ahem?' the fat man asks.

'I'm sorry, I thought somebody …' you say. 'I used to know the person who stayed here. I mean, I'm looking for somebody …'

Weeks pass, months pass, and he doesn't answer your calls until a year has gone by. And by then the void has already chewed off an essential part of you. In granting or withholding, human love has the same immense power: heal or bruise, keep sane or render insane, to wholly create or to completely destroy. Later, you gather yourself and sit on your bed and realise where you have gone wrong – that your primary objective ought to have been to protect yourself.

2.

Five years have gone by and one night in a club you meet Chuka, a DJ. You talk and talk and you talk some more. He follows South African music religiously. He lists Brenda Fassie's *Vulindlela* and Yvonne Chaka

Chaka's *Umqombothi* as his favourites, and insists that Nigerian pop music is mostly crap. It has good beats – in fact great beats – but poor lyrics: women, money, sex, parties, boats, women, boats, sex. It's never political, never deep thinking – except for three or four artists. 'Fela's spirit is gone, Onyeka Onwenu's spirit, Christy Igbokwe, all gone,' he says. You disagree on some points, but mostly agree, even though you're wary of his hasty conclusions. In the end, he plays you beats he has created, says he intends having D'banj record vocals on it. It is funky, with Afrobeats that begin with a splash of drums and then eases into mid-tempo with a hint of reggae. Chuka doesn't know anybody in the music industry; he intends to attend a D'banj show in Lagos and give it to him, beg him to listen to it, beg him for just a minute of his time to listen.

You want to ask him how he will ever get close enough to D'banj but you don't. Then it enters your head: 'How much will you sell it for?' you ask.

Chuka laughs. You can tell it's pity that he feels for you.

But then the world is a strange place and he ends up sending it to you. For free. On agreement that you have a one-week deadline to do something with it and play for him.

You write something, anything you think of: money, girls, money, girls, girls, even though you know it's not very good. You call it *Baby Mama*.

But Chuka likes it, says it's flat but still likes it. When you really think of it, he says, Nigerians suffer too much under the government to listen to heavy philosophy, to anything not light with good beats. But he isn't sure what to do with it – he's afraid that if it comes out a big artist might rip it off. Still he starts playing it in clubs, starts giving it to other DJs to play. You hover around night clubs hoping a few people will like it. A month passes before you hear from Chuka.

'You won't believe this!' he screams on the phone. 'Look, we totally have to redo this, but it will blow.'

You enter an okada and the motorcyclist speeds to Abia Polytechnic where Chuka is studying chemistry. You enter his flat and he introduces you to a friend, Jasper, a tall guy whose lavish looks contrast sharply with Chuka's unremarkable face. He's a writer freelancing for *The Sun* and *Premium Times*. You show Chuka what you have written down: new lyrics to *Baby Mama*. Jasper gives you ideas to make it a bit different, a bit more love and less shake-it-for-me, more life with a hint of desperation, like Djinee's *Ego*. It has to be a bit distinctive – or it will get drowned in the sea of songs out there. As you work, they chat about things – a new Genevieve Nnaji film, books, Rihanna's dress to a recent outing, a very creative artist called Wangechi Mutu, a Lady Gaga video – analysing and dissecting in that way of young people whose lives are defined only by their personal dreams and pop culture, yet spiced with long digressions by Chuka on politics, the world and why the world sucks. Suddenly Jasper asks, 'You don't follow politics?'

You shake your head, wondering if he's disappointed. You've never been interested in the questions they have flitted through: Why is Nigeria so fucked up? Why were Biafra's three million deaths allowed to happen? Why won't Biafra go away? How the heck did the Holocaust start? And Rwanda, Yugoslavia and Sudan – what devils rode into those places on horseback?

You wonder if it is selfish to simply not be interested, to be invested in only your own security. You are different from them. Fortunately, Jasper doesn't act as though you should know better, so you turn back to *Baby Mama*. You spend the next three hours in the sitting room writing, thinking, adding a few things. You need to urinate, so you walk towards the bedroom and push his door open, wanting to ask where the toilet is. And then you see them. Jasper is sitting astride Chuka. Both of them are bare-bodied. Jasper turns around slowly, confidently, like he doesn't care. Chuka bends his head. 'I'm sorry,' you say, backing out quickly, embarrassed.

A week later, Chuka calls and says, 'Tune in to BCA, they're playing it!'

It feels surreal hearing yourself on radio, your words floating on beats: *You've made me say I won't go, say I will stay, say you will be my baby, my mama!*

After the song ends, Chuka rings again and says, 'Guy, we made it!'

Things change. You change. People start to recognise your name. Chuka hires people to paste posters of you on walls and gates and electric poles along roads, and soon people begin recognising you on the road. Lavish hellos and shy waves. Clubs play *Baby Mama* non-stop. But there is still no money. One morning, as you walk out to wash your face, your neighbour, a slim man who is always in a wrapper, says, 'You're cursed.'

You stare at him. Papa Njideka doesn't talk to people. He spends his days sitting with his radio on his lap, looking out at Cemetery Road market in his singlet and wrapper.

'Your song is everywhere and you don't have money,' he says.

Inside your flat you cry. Your mother says, 'God does not disappoint.' She rubs your head and adds, 'You are destined to make it.'

It takes three months before Chuka calls to say you have a show at Terminus Hotel: a politician's birthday. You cry on the phone. 'We made it,' Chuka says again.

You make your first money six months after *Baby Mama* is out – a cool N200 000. Chuka says *Baby Mama* is taking over the east, he says people in Lagos are taking note. You and Chuka play more shows in Owerri and Onitsha and Enugu.

Then, one night, Chuka comes to your flat and says, 'Man, we have to move to Lagos.'

'Travel to Lagos?'

'We have to relocate to Lagos, Zukora,' he says, impatient at your lack of understanding of how these things work. He has everything worked out: he is now your manager; you two will stay with a friend of his, Akin, who knows a few radio DJs until something works out; you will have to befriend those DJs, and if the song blows, reach out to a major artist – Flavour or 2Face or P-Square or D'banj – for a remix. 'Aba is a city rotting away,' he says. 'Businesses are moving away. This place can never recover from that whole kidnapping thing in 2010.'

From the vibrant refuse-dump life of Aba's streets, with their open gutters, stagnant waters, potholes and roads that become rivers during the rains, to the stately, clean Victoria Island with its electrifying nightlife and the beautiful, lifeless mansions of Ajah tucked behind inordinately high estate fences, it is a drastic change of scenery. By the time you and Chuka settle into Akin's flat, into a room stuffed with dusty cartons, *Baby Mama* has blown. You play shows, mostly private ones for politicians and the newly wealthy Lagos Boys eager to be seen as having arrived. They don't appear to be tiring of the same song.

Your life changes. With money, life always changes. Chuka says you have to have a definite look, you can't afford to look generic. Everybody wears glasses but you won't – you'll have to define yourself so that you are known as you. Everybody you meet asks if you're working on an album and you say yes. Jasper gives you fresh ideas and you record six more songs. You decide the album will be about life, not just love, not just sex, but life. You put in a bit of Timaya: a story of how you arrived. You add a dash of WizKid: girls, money and young it-ness so you won't sound out of touch with your generation. You drop in some D'banj: full-blown Alpha male swagger, hormone-releasing charisma that proves you can handle it all and are in it for the long run. And finally you lace it with yourself, with how you actually feel. 'You can't afford to be entirely anybody's clone,' Chuka says, 'not even D'banj's.' You are in the studio when he says this and you look at him, this brainy man, once an acquaintance, now shaper of your life, and you ask, 'Are you really gay?'

You expect the question to knock him off, to dust off all that cool. It doesn't. He says, 'Yep.' Your question is not even grave enough to merit a proper yes. Since Dr Uzodinma six years back, you haven't been with any other man. It is a thirst that intensifies after each woman you meet, and lately you have started to feel as though you don't belong in your own skin.

'How many people know?' you say.

'Anybody I consider a friend,' he says.

All this time he doesn't bother looking up at you, is treating it as

117

just another chat he's used to. He gets up, paper cup in hand, places a hand on your shoulder, presses it and smiles. 'Let's run that hook again,' he says.

You will never forget that evening: his demeanour, your muted awe in that cramped studio. You will never forget because it is the last evening you will ever record something with him, ever hear his long speeches on Fela and Lucky Dube. Because after your album comes out and you become the staple of night clubs and day radio, after major artists begin lining you up for features and remixes and everybody begins talking about how you manage to both sing and rap well, after MOBO nominates you for that award that has Chuka screaming, 'I love you, man! I love you!', and after *The Fader* runs a profile on you and everybody begins talking about how you just might be the next poster boy of Naija pop, Chuka is attacked just outside a night club. He has a bottle broken on his head, pieces peeking out of his skull. In the hospital where you all surround him, Jasper cries and curses and curses some more. You find out that they broke up – this is the reason Chuka has looked increasingly confused and acted intensely distracted. But Chuka recovers. Things normalise and he resumes accompanying you to gigs, to awards nights, sitting beside you through interviews, a coy smile each time you say it's all down to your friend and manager.

And then …

He is found bleeding on the ground outside his apartment. There is a gash in his head, his teeth scattered everywhere. They say he jumped from the second-storey window. He dies. Chuka dies and your life will never be the same again. You skip food for days and lie crying on the floor, wondering whether telling him about yourself might have saved him.

Then one night you sit at your table and write *I Know*, but the song spins on the radio too much, it spins you into depression.

Two months after Chuka is gone, you decide to move back to Aba, to the duplex in Umuebeke where your mother now lives. Permanently.

3.

It is a year since Chuka died and you have a new manager, Nnamdi, recommended by a producer friend. He is an Aba boy like you, grown on the streets, tough as titanium under those suits and ties, very business-like. So business-like in your first meeting that you have to tell him something you don't want to tell any human being.

'I want a friend I can talk to sometimes, not just a business partner,' you say, holding his gaze until he darts his eyes to the floor and says with a quick nod, 'Okay.'

The two of you live in Aba, only visiting Lagos to do shows, mostly doing gigs in Awka or in Enugu where Flavour and Phyno run the show. You are back to doing private performances for political godfathers and billionaires, a few of whom want mentions in your songs, which you never give.

A week after the anti-gay law is signed, you perform in Abuja, the crowd shouting and screaming. You call up a girl, you stand with raised hands as she twerks on your zipper, twerk, twerk, twerk until the hall almost comes down with deafening loudness.

In addition to a new manager, you also have a new emptiness. A yawning pit, holes snaking through you, pent-up coarseness that craves an outlet. Daily, the hole sucks you in more. You fuck more than you usually do: girls from Abia Poly, girls at night gigs. Then one evening in your Port Harcourt hotel, just before a show, you meet him.

He is strange, Preye, not like anybody you've met before. Tall, dark, broad shoulders, tapering fingers, plump toes: a cliché of attractiveness working as a mechanic. Your driver brings him to your hotel room and stands there as he tells you about your Prado's faults. Afterwards, you ask him to leave his number. After they have left together, you call him and ask him to come back. He sits on the cushion and your gaze rests on his oil-flecked hands clasping a glass of red wine. The first feeling flushing up your chest is that you want to take him to the beach in Lekki. 'Are you, like, into guys?' you blurt out.

At first he seems not to have heard, then you see that he is frozen, approaching him. He lets you take his hand, he lets you help him onto the high bed, and he mumbles, 'Thank you.' You sit beside him. The room is wrapped in silence. There is a crack on his lower lip. You hold his hand, your fingers interlocking. You hold back the urge to shake uncontrollably.

One day you arrive early, but there is already a third person in the room. The man is fair-complexioned and wearing a cap and a sleeveless top with plain trousers. He is sitting on the bed, wearing slippers, and he and Doc are laughing at something on the laptop. 'He's made a new friend,' Chinelo says, with a tepid smile. You sit and watch them. Finally, you ask Chinelo: 'How have you been?'

You fall asleep on the chair and when you wake up the man is gone and Chinelo is asleep. Doc is staring into space. You take his hand. You touch his face and the back of your palm rests on the sprinkling of hair you haven't noticed until now. You wake Chinelo and tell her you won't be around for the next two weeks. London. Los Angeles. San Francisco. You have concerts – an international publicity tour for your second album. There is a look of helplessness on her face. 'Take care,' she finally says. You turn and look at him, then you open the door.

At home, in the sitting room, you sit at your mother's feet, your head on her lap. Her hands smell of groundnut soap, and somehow it makes you feel better. On the screen, Mercy Johnson is screaming at a man. 'This girl can act!' your mother says excitedly. It is almost the same pitch she used the day you tell her you're not sure you will marry. '*Ana m a tukwa anya nwa n'aka gi o!*' she snapped at you. Her acceptance of your nature hasn't altered her expectations of grandchildren. After she gets up, after she plants a kiss on your head, you get up and stagger into your room where you cry.

4.

You have too much material recorded for your second album. You have a lot of difficulty narrowing it down to eighteen tracks. Your sound is ambitious, a mix of genres – Afrobeats infused with reggae, house, South African music, eighties sounds and splashes of electronic dance – helmed by your Nigerian-Swedish producer DJ Wire. It is a risk. You have archetypes you want it to sound like: Cabo Snoop's *Windeck* banged up major attention in 2010; in 2012, D'banj's *Oliver Twist* crossed over to the UK charts; in 2013, Mafikizolo's *Khona* was king of radios across Africa and Davido's *Skelewu* was filling up dance floors from Lagos to Nairobi to Cape Town; in 2014, Lil Kesh's *Shoki* was tearing up the streets; and in 2015, it was WizKid's *Ojuelegba* that spread across the Atlantic.

Plus, you want to do an Afrobeats cover of Rihanna's *We Found Love*. All the time you work, the same playlist is on: Fela, Onyeka Onwenu, Olamide, Femi Kuti, Lucky Dube, Asa, Bob Marley, Adele, but mostly Rihanna's *Anti* album and Nicki Minaj. DJ Wire grew up on Lucky Dube. 'With reggae all things are possible,' he usually says, because he knows you will laugh. You draw up a list of artists you want on the record: Akon, Angelique Kidjo, Asa, D'banj, Flavour, Nneka, Phyno, Mafikizolo and Lil Kesh.

You are rushing the release; you can only rush it or push it back, and you don't want to push it back because Aba is on your mind.

You grant interviews where you reveal the album title: *The Emancipation of Fela*. It sounds too ambitious, journalists and bloggers are quick to point out. They want to know whether it will be political? Can it live up to its name? Is it metaphorical? Is your phase as one of Nigeria's most secretive celebrities about to be over? You ignore their questions, talk about its inspirations instead. 'There are a few love songs,' you tell them. 'Songs of hope also. It's inspired by a friend in need.' And you refuse to say more.

The Emancipation of Fela drops on a quiet Sunday while you're in Lagos. You're in your apartment when you post about its release to your 700 000 Twitter followers and 1.3 million Facebook fans.

And you break the Nigerian Internet.

5.

'Congratulations,' Chinelo says. It is a week later and you are visiting. The light bulb is flickering, your shadow darkening a large portion of the wall. The TV is on. 'Triple congratulations, actually,' she adds. You have been nominated at the BETs and the MOBOs. 'Thank you,' you say, smiling. You gesture at him. *'Kee ka o mere?'*

'He's improving. The doctor says it occasionally happens like that, and that sometimes the patient may break out of it.'

You nod slowly. She doesn't sound like she believes the doctor. False hope is the last thing anybody needs now.

She turns up the TV volume. 'In case you haven't noticed …' she says. The two women and one man on TV are discussing you:

'I mean, he's just different from the current crop of artists. He's had a blistering career so far – no scandals whatsoever, no silly posts on social media, no actual baby mama drama.' They burst into laughter. *'There's just something un-celebrity – if I could use that term – in his music. It's honesty. Yes, honesty and fierceness. His subject matter isn't about sex and partying and boasting; his message is urgent and so many people can relate to it. It might just be the soundtrack of this generation. I thought* Enyimba City *was just about Aba, but then my nephew says it's a love song! I think the best song there is* Teacher Fela.*'*

'I think your best song is *Wahala*. It's even better than *King of the Night*,' Chinelo says.

It never occurs to you to have a favourite song; you can't quite choose from among your children.

'Sometimes your voice is depressing, like it's serving up more than just the music. All your songs have that moment. It's as if you sing of a longing and there's a moment when it reveals itself,' she adds.

'We all have something we long for, something we wish didn't turn out the way it has.'

She is at the window, drawing the curtain. When she turns, you say, 'I am in love. It's been the same person for most of my life.'

It is when she doesn't look at you, doesn't do anything to show that she heard you, that you suddenly remember: the person you love is her father. She still doesn't look at you. She is dressing her father's bed; her manner too deliberate in its avoidance of this new subject. You ignore her unease. 'That's what makes life life,' you say.

The only thing wrong with love is the lovers. After you leave in your Jeep that night, after you pass Port Harcourt Road where, from a busy bar, Hozier's *Take Me to Church* filters into the night, his voice raising the hair on your skin, your driver stops at Asa Triangle Road and whispers, 'Sir?' as he stretches his hand and holds your kneecap because you've begun sobbing and shaking. You hold your head and say, '*Onwero. Onwero*. I just dey tired. I wan shag this night. Go to Ama Awusa.' You catch his suspicious stare in the rear-view mirror. After you lie under the small-hipped girl whose braids are so long they rest on your chest and you thrash around like never before, agitatedly, sloppily, you surrender completely to the tension rushing up from your feet and down from your brain and fingers.

The next evening you go to the hospital. You enter the room and see him sitting next to the man with the cap. They look up and look back down at the laptop and, for the first time, it occurs to you that the man with the cap is young, in his thirties maybe. The young man shrieks with laughter. Just after his laugh dies down, Doc looks up again. He slowly pushes the laptop to the young man and stands up. He starts out towards you. His eyes on yours. You feel dissolution, a swirl of emotions. You feel hot tears on your face. Then halfway between his bed and you, Doc stops. He turns and goes back. He sits beside the man whose blank eyes have been on you all along, and together they look back at the laptop and burst out laughing.

You are standing there, in the centre of the room, crying. It is overwhelming. The ephemeral return of his memories was so overwhelming that you leave. You sit alone in your car and return minutes later. Chinelo opens the door when you knock, comes out and closes it behind her. 'I think my father is getting better,' she says, leaning on the white wall of the passage, hands folded, a wrenched smile on her face. You see that she has again taken up the risk of hoping, that she has not given up, like you have.

'I think so, too,' you say.

'I want to ask something of you,' she says. You hear the words before she says them. You think of looking down as she says them but you still stare. 'Please don't come back here,' she says.

You try to sound calm. 'Why?'

'Please do not make things hard for us all by pushing this.'

You stare at her for a while. She is right. It is gratitude you owe her for allowing you to see him in the first place.

'I love him. I have loved him since I was nine years old. I have looked up to him since my father died. He is like a second father to me.'

'You love him.' She is nodding slowly. 'He is like a second father to you.'

'For me to say this, you have to know how much I mean it.'

'So?' Her eyes meet yours. 'You're gay. So?'

Even though you're the one to imply it, the word still throws you off balance and makes your heart jump. Dryness spreads in your throat. You are staring at her. You do not know how to take this. Something is breaking in you, throwing itself up, snapping in half. Something in you is giving way. Your palm rests on the wall.

Love, in essence, is tenancy.

'Will you call me if he recovers?'

'It doesn't change anything,' she says.

You turn.

You stagger back up the passage, which now seems burnished with white light.

You hear her open the door and then hear it close.

In the days that follow, the world will be bandaged in fog. You will be soaked in a numbing ache and your mother will hold you in her lap like a baby. She will whisper: 'I raised a brave man.' You will get calls from colleagues saying how courageous you are. Jasper, holding you in a hug and holding back tears, will say, 'Chuka would be so proud of you.' The telecommunications company you're endorsing will call to ask what your plans are because they're afraid you'll drive away customers, but they're also afraid to lose you. Nnamdi will turn down every interview request and deactivate your Facebook page and you'll see in his eyes that he is unsure, that what you have done might break your career. In those coming days, Preye will text you: *I don't know if you still use this number but I heard. You're strong – not like me. I just want to let you know that nobody ever made me feel so cared for until you. Good luck.* And you'll text him your address. And he'll show up in two hours, all clean in his suit, and you'll throw your body at him in a hug. When you disentangle from him, you see that his eyes are reddened. 'Do you have any plans?' he will ask later that evening, seated, his palms pressed together. You will shake your head.

All of this will happen in the coming days.

But now, on the hospital staircase, you almost fall down on the rough edges of the steps. The thing clutching your throat will not let go. When you slip on the last step you're already crying. You sit there and wail. You are surrounded by nurses and one offers you a chair in an office where you sit alone, wiping your tears. She stays with you and is standing there as you bring out your phone, as you type words slowly. You're in a haze. You stare at the words.

You tweet three words: *I am homosexual.*

The conversation

OLAKUNLE OLOGUNRO

BEFORE I FOUND OUT THE MEANING of the word effeminate, I was already aware of how much of a girl I was. Then, I would have given a finger to become a dancer in a pop video, to paint my lips and wear wigs that reached my waist. It was there, in my voice, in the hours I spent preening in front of our living room mirror that was framed with green plastic. It was in the lip gloss I used because if I didn't wear it my lips would dry out. It was in my mother's dresses, the ones I tried on when she was away.

In school, I was called girlish-boy. My classmates said my hips swayed when I walked. They said I could fling my arms and make more exaggerated gestures than most – if not all – the girls in my class. Later, they called me Canary or Nightingale because no matter how hard I tried, my voice never had the bass of the other boys, only the delicate wavering of a song.

Sometimes I would force out the baritone to hear how the male voice sounded coming from my lips but I knew as I produced the sounds that it wasn't mine, that it was not what I wanted to be. I knew I liked boys when I got an erection the day my uncle took a bath with me. His penis grazed my back when he scrubbed my leg. I was seven and aware of an alien rush of feelings in me; they made goose bumps form on my skin. But I had no name for it. I didn't know that there was a tag, an identity for this feeling. I didn't know there were others like me, people who looked at naked uncles and felt a stirring deep in their bodies.

I was nine when our neighbour's son kissed me. It was a simple thing and ought to be have been treated as such – just a touch of lips because we wanted to play, and there was no one to imitate mother. Yet there was no simplicity in the response I felt in my penis, which strained against the fabric of my yellow cotton underpants with their elastic band. This kiss was followed by others. We played often and the suggestion of 'let's act like I'm sleeping on you' was made with increasing frequency. His family moved away in 2005, the year the Bellview plane crashed. I remember his chipped front tooth. I remember not wanting them to go.

There were others after him. There was Mayowa, the one who was always behind the fence after darkness had fallen. There was Chibuike, the pastor's son who interpreted every Sunday sermon and shouted like his father. Then there was Austine, the one with the penis that leaked with just one touch, and John with the body odour and faded Arsenal jersey.

I was eager to discover, hungrily taking in but not sure of when to give. But I grew more certain. After each sweaty kiss, each slippery fumble with a new lover, I understood more about my body – I knew that my body's displays of lust were as personal as my skin. No matter which guy I happened to be attracted to, this was who I was: a gay man.

I met Ibrahim when I went to university. It was the year I decided to live without conforming, to open up and be free. University was nothing like I had expected it to be. The lecture theatre had broken seats and dangerously twisted metal jutted out of the places where the seats had fallen off. The windows had too much dust and the boards hadn't been cleaned properly, their white surfaces marred with faded writing that had been scribbled over too many times. On the day I met Ibrahim, I was shouting at a taxi driver. The driver was shouting back. Ibrahim, a dark-skinned guy in a cocaine-white shirt and distressed denim, intervened. He said a careful, 'It's okay, *e mabinu*,' and paid the taxi driver. He turned and offered me a ride in his vanilla-scented car. He was privileged: he owned a car and lived alone. Whereas my parents asked incessant questions, calculated my pocket money and rationed my foodstuffs. That you are in university does not give room for wastage, they said often. And remember who your father is. No one seemed to be asking Ibrahim questions and lecturing him.

Ibrahim met my parents when we had Christmas break. Something had formed between us then, an elaborate collection of emotions and need. We had gone past the awkward stage of getting to know each another. I wanted Ibrahim, and he wanted me. It did not matter how or why. With Ibrahim I felt an assured security, like I could stand on a table with broken legs and never fall, like I could leap from a great height and land in the safety of his arms. He and my father bonded because my father was pleased that I had made friends with a fellow Muslim and an older person who could act as a guardian and make sure I never misbehaved. My mother called him respectful, laughed at his jokes, asked about his family and insisted that he eat. Would he like some *fura* or did he prefer *beske*? I sat demurely across from them in the living room, and watched as though they were actors that I loved in a play. This was happiness – never mind that the premise was a lie.

After their meeting, my parents gave their approval freely. Yes, you can move in with him. Of course you can spend *sallah* at their place. Give Alhaja this hijab for me. Tell her *barka se sallah*. It was too normal, too harmless-looking to attract questions.

The first time Ibrahim slapped me was a Tuesday. I remember how dusty that day was. Earlier that day, I had gone for a lecture that was cancelled because the lecturer could not find fuel. Since going back home would be a waste of money, I spent the afternoon with my friends, talking about forgiveness and laughing about how annoying it was that MTN had to make their customers register one SIM card a hundred times. It was nightfall by the time I got home. I got in and said, 'Babe, what's up?' He was reading a book. He liked to read in the evenings. Better assimilation, he'd once said when I asked him why. An empty cup sat on the table as though he were royalty. 'What were you doing in school that kept you so long?' he asked without looking up. I put down my bag, reached for the cup, filled it with water and drank before I answered.

'Just the normal. You know our school.' I flopped down on the mattress.

'That doesn't answer my question.'

I turned to look at him. He dropped the book and faced me. A tuft of wool from the pillow was trapped in his hair.

'What happened?' I asked, sitting up.

'I called someone in your department and she told me you guys had no lecture today, so what were you doing in school till this time?'

I exhaled and smiled. 'I like it when you are jealous. It makes me feel special.'

I stood up to start on dinner but he stood in my way. I stopped, taken aback. He had never acted this way before.

'Where. Are. You. Coming. From?' He asked with a deliberate slowness. His voice – lowered so people from the next room would not hear him – had taken on an ominous cadence.

I frowned. 'Where else?'

The rest of my sentence was disrupted by the slap. I felt his palm on my cheek. It was heavy as though it was not simply a hand. I was dumbfounded. I gaped at him in shock. In all the months of our relationship – months of sex and gentle whispers, months when the dusty wind settled on clean pots and plates and heavy rains saw us pulling the curtains close and falling asleep in each other's arms – he had never slapped me.

I found my voice. I spoke slowly. It felt like someone was borrowing my body, speaking with my voice and using my brain, like the real me was still at school and this was merely a shell standing in front of Ibrahim.

I said his name but nothing else would come out. 'Ibrahim.' The power of coherent speech eluded me. Words were like birds scattering to escape the stones of a child's catapult.

'You are no longer who you used to be,' he said and went out, slamming the door behind him.

After he left, I touched my cheek again to make sure what happened was real, that I had not imagined it. Everything in the room still seemed normal and this surprised me. The curtains fluttered insouciantly. Someone from the next room laughed. The cup sat innocently on the table. Perhaps he was angry about something else, I told myself, but even then the stupidity of the statement glinted at me darkly. Still, I assured myself that was it. I was feeding myself a false truth I desperately needed to believe.

Ibrahim did not come home that night. He returned the next morning just as the noise of the morning prayer call from the mosque was pushing against the windows.

'I'm sorry,' he said.

I stared at him. There were things I could have done, words I could have shouted at him. Instead I stared at him in silence. The women in the room next to ours were praying, their cries of 'Jehovah!' and 'Lord Jesus!' sounded like words of strife rather than words of peace.

He reached for my hands and held them in his. I shook them away.

'Sorry I acted that way. I'm really sorry. I don't know what came over me, I swear.'

It became a mime: his voice saying sorry, his hands squeezing mine gently and his lips on mine. It moved into a kiss and then there was the urgency of need, of unsaid apologies, binding us together. It was there in his thrusts, in his moans, in our muffled voices bleeding into each other. Afterwards, he slipped out and unrolled the soiled condom. We showered. He went to join the morning prayers.

The next time he hit me was a week later. A classmate, a male who Ibrahim said had the tendencies of being gay the first day they met, had called me. Ibrahim and I had been cuddling in bed when the phone rang. I disengaged from him so I could pick up the call. It was a simple question of 'did the lecturer for BCH 212 say he would be there at 2pm or not?' which got a direct 'no' and then the call moved on to how annoying the lecturers were and how tiring our school was and how it seemed like final year and graduation was a lifetime away and why we needed to have a new course rep. A minute passed, then two, then five, and we were still on the phone, laughing and exchanging annoying instances of mistreatment of students by lecturers. Ibrahim stood up, filled a glass, gulped it, parted the curtains, flipped through a textbook and closed it again, then finally snatched the phone from me and ended the call.

'What is the meaning of this *one na*, Ibrahim?' I asked. Outside the window, a pepper seller trudged by. Her wrapper was green, the light green of a beer bottle.

'Oh,' he said in the way that one does to draw attention to a ridiculous thing. 'So it has now got to the point where your lover can call you at home, ehn?'

I laughed. 'Lover indeed. Since when did you and I become married that I should have a lover?'

The phone began to ring again. I stood up and reached for it on the bed.

'Pick up that call and I'll show you what I can do,' he said.

I laughed. He often joked with things like that, usually the 'what he could do' ending up as kisses and sex. 'You have taken something, I know. Hello *jare*,' I said and placed the phone to my ears.

The force of the slap pushed the phone from my hands. It landed on the floor in pieces. I was stunned into silence.

'So I've taken weed, *abi*?' He did not wait for an answer. His slaps descended on my face, the dryness of his palm sweeping across my lips.

'Ibrahim!' I winced, but he silenced me. A punch on my back, on my face. He was speaking and hitting me at the same time.

'You are nothing but a fucking slut, fucking guys when I am not around.' A punch. 'You think I don't know? You think I don't?' Another punch.

I struggled but I could not get rid of him. I reached for his shirt and held the neck, slackened it. I wished I were as masculine as he was, I wished I weren't effeminate so I could match his punches with mine and draw blood. He finally stopped, breathing heavily. I knew I had to leave then. I knew I had to pack up what remained of my dignity and never look back.

I was sore when I woke up the next morning. I had a cut on my lower lip and a throbbing headache. When I went into the bathroom to take a bath, Ibrahim was praying, the ends of his jellabiya grazing the floor. It seemed ironic that he could pray with such serenity after what happened. Still, neither of us were strangers to irony. After all, since we met we often prayed then fucked, with Ibrahim saying '*Alhamdullilahi*' as he slipped out of me and unrolled the condom.

Everyone wanted to know why I had a swollen lip.

'You will not believe,' I said, 'thieves came to our hostel yesterday. In fact, my roommate had to go to the clinic to get a bandage. He was badly beaten!' We were under a cashew tree beside the lecture theatre. A colony of honey-coloured ants marched down its callused trunk.

'Thieves, in this area?' Amaka asked, surprised.

'I'm very sure it will be those new students or those jobless guys in this area,' Deolu said. Everyone laughed. I could not tell him it was his call that gave me a swollen lip and an aching body.

'But you sef, you dull o! When you go dey do like woman,' Iyke said. He was the oldest in our department and had a hairy chest and a clean-shaven head. He had never spoken normal English. 'Thief come your villa, you no fit attack them. Your matter tire me o. If na to talk who sabi sing for Rihanna and Beyoncé now, na you go dey scream.'

I smiled, embarrassed. But there was no way I could stand up to Ibrahim. I could never match him. In secondary school, I carefully avoided fights with the guys and paired with the girls. It was easier to say, 'I don't beat girls,' or engage in a battle of slaps and clapping hands with them if the worst came to be.

When I returned home, Ibrahim was on the phone. I walked past him and lay down on the bed.

'Your mum wants to speak with you,' he said and handed the phone to me. I took it without looking at him.

'Hello.'

'Ahmed, so you have started walking with bad boys, *abi*?' My mother said entirely in Yoruba. She did not reply to my hello.

'Ma? Who told ...' I began.

'Shut up! Ibrahim is lying, *abi*? You're now in second year and think you can do what you want, *abi beeko*? *Ika kan o wo e n'di mo*! You think you are now independent, *abi*?'

I was angry. Since when did my mother start to value the opinion of others and not mine?

'But you should listen to me and hear my own side now, Mummy.'

'What is there to hear?'

I breathed heavily and glared at Ibrahim.

'Be careful, Ahmed. Be very careful. It is your gourd that will point where it will be tied to. Give the phone to Ibrahim.'

I knew then that I was fighting a lost battle, that I was trapped in an airless room. I wondered how long I could stay before I passed out.

I shouldn't have remained with Ibrahim but I did. I stayed until life became a cycle: beat, make up, remain. I hated watching my soul melt away, but I stayed because he had the same tag as I did: he was gay. I had no one to talk to about him, no friends who were gay and understood what it felt like to be restricted to only one option, nobody who would listen to me say I was gay without wanting to throw a tyre round my neck and burn me or want to parade me naked saying I was a disgrace.

I stayed because nobody believed that abuse could happen in a gay relationship. My friend Asantewa, whose sister had recently divorced her husband who liked to hit her, said in her Ghanian-accented English that such things only happened in straight relationships. 'I mean,' she had said that slow June day while brushing her hair out of face, 'why would a guy even date a guy in the first place? He deserves to have some sense beaten into him.'

I took her words in silence the same way I took Ibrahim's abuse in silence. The slap at the bus stop, the yank at the ear for talking to a guy at ShopRite, the damaging of my SIM card, the violent sex that left me sore and bleeding, and the tears in the bathroom. I never told anyone and I never fought back. Once, he burnt my shirt because he said a guy bought it for me. Once, he flogged me with a belt because I refused to have sex with him. How could I be tired? Just how? I had gone to fuck another guy, right? I wanted to leave him, right? And afterwards, he would buy me medicine, cook me dinner or lunch, do the laundry and say, '*Astaghfirullah.*' And I would remain. Then he would pray. He never missed any of the prayer hours.

I left him when I realised I couldn't take it anymore. It was the third year of our relationship and there were only months till his final papers. I simply picked up my school books and left. I still had one more year to go but that didn't matter. I left my phone and new SIM card in his place, left everything he bought me, which was almost everything I had. I decided that if God would kill me, then it should not be at the hands of someone who was supposed to love me.

My mother was aghast. Why would I leave my best friend of all these years for no reason? My father, too. Ibrahim sent countless messages, got my new number from my mother and wouldn't stop texting, asking what he did wrong and why I left. My mother would not hear of it, but I told her one night: 'If a stranger can make you lose trust in your child, then I wonder why you call me your child in the first place.'

It was that night my father knew they were knocking on a closed door. 'Leave him alone, *Ummuani*,' he told my mother. 'Didn't you hear him?'

I took control of my own life when I realised the person I trusted it to was kicking it around like a ball. But it took me three years. Three years of being raped, three years of taunts and jeers, three years of tears, three years of chasing empty air, three years of everlasting scars. It took me that long. It took three years because I knew that I couldn't say a word as no one wanted to listen. It took me three years because I knew no one cared to ask whether I was limping to be fashionable or because I had a thorn underfoot.

There was a long silence after my monologue, but I knew. I had expected it. What I had not expected, though, was the lightness I felt in my soul after telling her. She reached in her handbag and brought out a tissue.

'Here,' she said.

'Oh.' I was not aware of the tears sliding down my cheeks. But I was aware of the cool evening breeze on my arms. 'Thank you.'

'You know, my fiancé was like that too.' She licked her lips and studied her nails that were painted a shimmery grey.

'He was?'

'Yes. But no one cared. My people were more interested in marrying me off. Even when I came home with a bruise, my mother would say, "Stay, Labake, stay. When you get married, you'll pray for God to change him." And each time I called her to complain, she would say, "Look, no man is perfect. It is you who will build him to be the kind of man you want. People are talking, they say you have expired."'

I glanced at her hands to see if there was a ring. I was not sure I saw one earlier. She caught my glance and smiled.

'I left.'

'You left?' I turned to look at her.

'Yes, I did. On the morning of my wedding. I had already dressed and was looking at my future with him. But I didn't like what I saw. So I left. The hairdresser was sorting out hair oils, the caterers were slaving away in the backyard and guests were being seated, but there was no bride. It was a major scandal. I thought the world would end.'

'Oh, I'm so sorry.'

She chuckled, a brave chuckle, the chuckle of someone who has moved on from something and did not need sympathy anymore.

'Don't be. I realised I owned my *own* life. But of course that realisation took a lot from me. My parents severed all ties with me, and I can't attend our family church without hearing snide remarks.' She sighed. 'Yesterday, I ran into my mother at the mall and she simply walked past me and continued shopping.' Her voice began to quiver. 'I was hurt because I thought she would understand. She is my mother, after all.' She sniffed and dabbed at her nose elegantly.

I moved closer and held her in my arms in an embrace that said I understood. She smelled of delicate innocence.

'My parents don't know I'm gay and are expecting grandchildren. I wonder what will happen when they find out.'

'You can leave too, you know,' she said and burst out laughing. I stared at her first and then joined in the laughter, our voices rising.

'But it would never be the same,' she said still laughing. Her laughter trickled into chuckles and then it stopped and she became quiet.

'No, it wouldn't,' I agreed after a while.

I don't know who began to cry first, but soon there were tears running down my cheeks and there were sobs escaping her throat, and we cried as though we were one person – a soul split into two bodies but a single unit nonetheless. Strangers stared and we did not care. We were who we were: an effeminate man in an Ankara caftan and an elegant woman in a banana-coloured dress sitting on a park bench crying. Together.

Stranger in familiar land

SARAH WAISWA

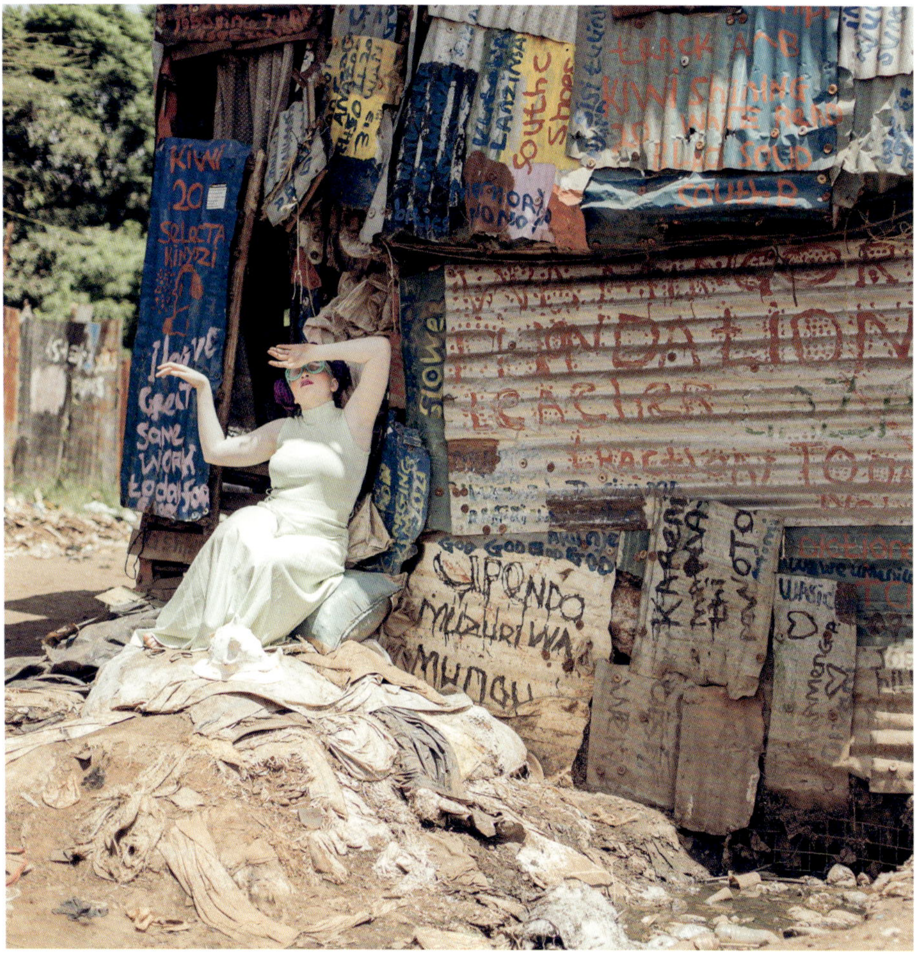
KIWI
20
Great
Same
WORK
slower

One more nation bound in freedom
Themes from the Nigerian anti-gay law

AYODELE SOGUNRO

IRONIES AND DICHOTOMIES

THE TITLE OF THIS PIECE is partly lifted from the first stanza of the Nigerian national anthem. The unintended irony in the phrase is a demonstration of Nigeria's dalliance with contrasting philosophies and a generic – if simplified – explanation for the emergence of anti-LGBT legislation in the country, despite the absence of any public crisis on the issue.

Nigeria has always suffered from an overdose of ironic circumstances. This is evident in its inception as a geopolitical amalgamation of two distinct socio-political administrations – now *bound in freedom* – and in the current international perception of Nigerians as resourceful yet not-quite-trustworthy people. This irony permeates every stratum of Nigerian psychology, creating contrasting influences and generating continuous tension between the developmental resources available to the country and the negative fallouts from its historical – traditional, colonial and national – biases, finally culminating in a social stasis – an orbital lock, you may say – that has left Nigeria at socio-political maturity level no higher than that which it possessed on October 1, 1960, when it gained its independence.

This is no flippant statement. Nigeria has neither progressed by reference to economic or socio-political indices (especially in the way that a number of other Commonwealth countries have), nor has the country *actually* disintegrated – the civil war notwithstanding – at least, not in the way that observers have forecasted since the late 1960s.

Today, the recent passage of the Same Sex Marriage (Prohibition) Act (the anti-gay law, for convenience) is not excluded from the ironic and contrastive Nigerian social psychology. This persistent social psychology makes it clear that there is never a single Nigerian answer to any question of policy; and an external observer would be properly astonished at the range of contrasting social themes that, as the anti-gay law has demonstrated, could eventually emerge as another bewildering aspect of Nigerian public policy. The following paragraphs highlight some of the social and legal themes that propel the peculiar enactment of a law that 'in so few paragraphs directly violates so many basic, universal human rights', as Navi Pillay, United Nations Commissioner for Human Rights 2008–2014, observed.

RELATIONSHIPS: SEX OR MARRIAGE?

The principal intent of the law, eponymously self-evident, is the prevention of homosexual marriages in Nigeria. But consider the following argument:

Fact 1: Marriage is necessarily a socio-legal system-sanctioned arrangement.
Fact 2: The existing socio-legal systems in Nigeria are incompatible with a homosexual relationship.
Fact 3: The anti-gay law exists.

Conclusion 1: The anti-gay law seeks to prevent a type of marital relationship that is already incompatible with the existing socio-legal system.
Conclusion 2: The anti-gay law erves no purpose for marital relationships under the Nigerian socio-legal systems.

The foregoing is as valid an analysis as one can manage if solely focused on the marriage issue. But the second conclusion above remains valid *only* if one believes that the principal intent of the law is the prevention of homosexual marriages in Nigeria. However, no Nigerian really believes that. The recent court cases in Nigeria indicate that the law is not about preventing same-sex marriage, instead it is about preventing – or more accurately, punishing – same-sex intercourse and, more broadly, homosexual *identity*. But a law that claims only to be against 'same-sex marriage' sounds nicer. Because, you see, Nigerians are nice people.

FOUNDATIONS: WHAT CULTURE, WHAT RELIGION?

The most common rationale for the anti-gay law is that homosexuality is anathema to both Nigerian culture and religion. However, consider this: the Nigerian cultural identity comprises up to 250 (or 102, depending on your criteria) ethnicities with carrying, and sometimes opposing, cultural norms, most of which have been sacrificed at the altars of Nigeria's main religious identities – Christianity and Islam. The argument that homosexuality is not a part of the Nigerian cultural heritage therefore becomes subject to ridicule when one considers the variety of cultural norms in Nigeria, and the dismissive treatment casually meted out to these cultural norms after the advent of Christianity and Islam.

This leaves us with the religious argument, and in Nigeria, that is an argument to be respected – somewhat. Probably no other country in the world takes as much pride in its public piety as Nigeria does. Public and private functions, whether commercial or non-profit, are commenced and ended with prayers. The church industry is 'big business', one whose annual turnover – if such measures exist – would rival those of the banking and telecommunications industries. The Islamic oligarchy is in firm control of the north, and in the south, the mere title of *Alhaji* – one who has gone on a pilgrimage to Mecca – is treated with maximum social respect. There are many more examples of Nigeria's religious bedrock: its permutations are endless.

Yet Nigeria is listed as a high-ranking corrupt officialdom, its elections are consistently flawed, and carriers of its passport are universally suspected. In fact, displays of moral extremism and religious fanaticism are not considered to be socially acceptable virtues in Nigeria. Even the introduction of the Sharia legal system in certain parts of the north was generally opposed, and it only became tolerable after the explanation that its application was *via* the personal choice of law of the litigants, or the accused. Across the country, the entertainment industry has a materialistic nature, and a Hollywood-style philosophy permeates the pop culture.

Thus, one could argue that the religious nature of the country is superficial, rather than principled – and this hypocrisy is generally tolerated in everyday Nigerian life. Consequently, it is highly uncharacteristic by Nigerian standards for a religious argument to be the prop for any governmental regulation, or worse, federal law, and more so when the constitution of the country unequivocally disavows a state religion.

In short, acceptance of the religious argument in support of the anti-gay law requires a convenient disregard of the amoral religiosity of Nigerian society. It would then be an error of judgement for an observer to fail to challenge this rationale, especially on a premise that Nigerians scrupulously desire a theocratic legal system. If such a fantastic idea were to be implemented, the political, administrative and commercial structure of the country would crash. And every Nigerian knows this.

A Nigerian politician may cheerfully announce to his audience that the passage of the anti-gay law is a reflection of the wishes of the majority of Nigerians. Considerations about the fairness of majority numeric strength versus minority human rights aside, such a statement would still be incorrect. While it is true that a great number of Nigerians are religiously, and to an extent culturally, *disapproving* of homosexual relationships, there also exist a fair number of such disapproving Nigerians who believe that public interference in private consenting sexuality is not within legislative competence. These Nigerians believe the law to be a greater evil than the sexuality it seeks to curb. There are no existing statistics to gauge the exact percentage of these Nigerians, but this much is clear: the legislative philosophy that birthed the law did not account for this category. To sum it up, Nigerians in general tend to adopt a 'live and let live socio-cultural philosophy', and while the majority of Nigerians are clearly not in support of homosexuality, not all of these Nigerians are directly anti-homosexual or homophobic.

CRIMINAL JURISPRUDENCE: COLONIAL LEGACY OR MODERN DEMOCRACY?

Nigeria's criminal law, excepting public corruption offences and commercial law offences, is cryogenically embalmed in a colonial pod. A few states, like Lagos, often review these colonial relics and upgrade them to meet modern social requirements, but overall the criminal legal system, and its underlying jurisprudence, remains essentially unmodified from their British shape.

Accordingly, the general Nigerian criminal code is peppered

with Victorian-era morality, crudely adapted to local conditions by the colonial government to ensure proper administration and resulting in ridiculous propositions such as the allowance of corporeal punishments, misogynist limitations of certain criminal responsibility, and, of course, the infamous series of 'unnatural offences', including this, which somehow weds sexism to incomprehensible legalese:

> ... any person who permits a male person to have *carnal knowledge* of him or her *against the order of nature* ... is guilty of a felony, and is liable to imprisonment of seven years.

The law has no definition of what exactly constitutes 'order of nature', and the interpretation is left to the personal tolerance of the trial judge.

This 19th-century punitive criminal system was further amplified by the long years of military rule and repressive policies. Under the recurrent military regimes, legislative authority is derived from the decrees of the military 'head of state' – and a crime was simply what the head of state declared to be a crime, even if retroactively. As a rule, the military had no use for, in the infamous words of then-General Buhari, 'the nonsense of legal proceedings'.

With this historical excursion in view, it is easy to see how Nigeria's criminal jurisprudence is largely punitive and repressive in nature. Reformative criminal laws are a novelty, and individual liberty within the social context is almost non-existent in the criminal law jurisprudence. Set in tension with this is the fact that constitutional democracy – as entrenched in the current Nigerian constitution – is much more tolerant than the criminal laws will allow. However, while very few Nigerians are familiar with the principles of constitutional democracy (particularly because of its relatively recent application in 1999), almost every politically conscious Nigerian is aware of the punitive philosophy embedded in the criminal laws. That punitive ideology often flares up as mob violence in situations where the orchestrators have low confidence in the adequacy of the criminal justice system. Consequently, most Nigerians are, by long usage, quite tolerant of a punitive and brutal criminal justice system – whether legal or illegal – and would, therefore, not think of the anti-gay law as a strange legal development.

The foregoing, though, does not detract from the fact that Nigerians yearn for a proper, modern constitutional government. Nigerians, generally, are believers in human rights as they construe them – especially in police-citizen interactions. Furthermore, Nigerians are strong believers in democratic government: they are incurable optimists in their certainty of the possibility of good governance. In everyday governance and public administration, Nigerians are prime pushers for 'equal opportunity', to the extent of their understanding of this concept. Evidence of this democratic spirit is the energy and resources that are invested by both the government and private citizens in developing democratic institutions within the country – even if superficially. Nigerians, at least at the moment, don't want a return to military rule – that bogeyman that lurks in the wings, constantly utilised by the media as a warning for errant politicians – and its attendant disciplinarian principles.

It is merely another example of the familiar irony that, while Nigerians are keen to have a Western-style democratic government, they are largely unschooled in – or unwilling to accommodate – the principles of liberty and equality that make such a government possible.

IDENTITY: NEO-COLONIALISM AND NATIONALISM

A recurrent theme prior to and after the passing of the anti-gay law has been the struggle to constitute an internationally acknowledged Nigerian identity, and the hope that the enforcement of anti-homosexual laws will contribute to the development of this identity. In the anti-gay Nigerian movement, this impulse is articulated in the assertion that homosexuality is a Western importation, and should therefore be kicked out of the country. The identity argument is closely linked to, but cannot be entirely conflated with, cultural arguments. Whereas cultural arguments are specifically about the continuation of an imagined African heritage, the identity argument is a response to perceived threats of neo-colonialism from the West.

Of course, a number of Nigerian legislators are geopolitically knowledgeable enough to understand that homosexuality exists in the Middle and Far East – as it does in the West – and also that strong homophobic sentiments are as pervasive in the West as everywhere else. Still, the few who brandish this nationalism argument treat the country's legislative capacity as a sort of nuclear weapon, the exhibition of which gives the country a definite identity and an improved status in the international realm. These are Nigerians who insist that the West can receive and accommodate Nigerian homosexuals if it is that desirous of allowing homosexuals liberties, or, in a supposedly fair but misguided attempt at negotiation, that the West should recognise polygamy in exchange for the recognition of gay marriages.

This argument gained even more traction with the threat of sanctions against Nigeria by Western democracies after the presidential assent to the law. In fact, any such international sanctions against Nigeria will most likely be seen as justifying this argument, and consequently elevate the anti-LGBT political elements to martyr status. A few proponents of this argument have considered China a suitable economic partner for the 'new' Nigeria, in an environment free of the 'human rights' apron strings of the West. Nigeria is fond of 'flexing' political muscles, and any perceived injury to the ego of the West – sticking it to the man – is enough to inspire a feel-good political atmosphere, so long as no real damage is done to foreign diplomatic relations. Nigerians, including the identity-seeking intelligentsia, are generally hospitable to Western influences. They just don't like the influences to be forced on them.

But human rights are universal – whether or not a specific geopolitical entity chooses to recognise these rights. Accordingly, the identity argument is, of course, absurd. The homosexual debate is not a new Cold War, and there are no political ideologies that bind the LGBT community. Not all members of the international LGBT community believe in the universal applicability of human rights – or perceive that there is even a 'gay community' of which to speak.

SOCIO-POLITICAL ISSUES: POLITICAL DISTRACTION OR SOCIAL GOOD?

Let us be clear about this: there is no homosexual 'problem' in Nigeria. There is no 'gay lobby', and there is no society-wide LGBT crisis. Very few Nigerians have direct interaction with members of the LGBT community. The LGBT community is necessarily private in Nigeria – private enough that, barely a decade ago, President Obasanjo was bold enough to publicly declare that there were no homosexuals in Nigeria! Furthermore, it is generally conceded by the current legislature that the law isn't meant to solve an existing situation, but to prevent a potential one – a *pre-emptive strike* against the gay marriage lobby. The question then arises: why this particular issue? Why not issues of urgent national importance?

A generous answer will suggest that the homosexuality issues are a 'simple' issue that can be easily fixed – and the alarming shoddiness of the few paragraphs that constitute the law almost make this a worthy answer. However, Nigerians politicians have little reputation for altruistic behaviour, and healthy scepticism leads up to the conclusion that the anti-gay law is merely a political distraction – a sleight of hand – calculated to eclipse the general incompetence of the legislature in addressing fundamental issues of governance.

The current political gameplay has a historical precedent too. The Ghana-must-go anti-immigrant legislative episode of the Shehu Shagari civilian regime in the 1980s was also a desperate attempt by the government to shift focus from the corrupt government and its responsibility for the economic decline after the oil boom of the 1970s. The trick was to blame the Ghanaians in the country instead.

Nigerians, who ordinarily are hospitable people, fell for this bogus explanation and – in anticipation of a renewed economic growth – jubilated publicly at the expulsion of the Ghanaian immigrants.

CONCLUSION

This is what an international observer needs to understand about Nigeria and its anti-gay law: the law has arisen from a kaleidoscope of contrasting elements in the Nigerian social and legal psyche. The laws are an anomaly in a country of anomalies – and the double negative transforms it into a supposedly positive necessity for the polity. It is hard to put a finger on any one reason for the emergence of the legislation; it is definitely not *just* a clear issue of morality, not a new wave of anti-Western ideology, not a backlash against an existing homosexual rights lobby, not anything in particular. In fact, the whole venture defies propositional logic, but only to a non-Nigerian.

For the heterosexual majority of Nigerians, the passage of the law is not a fundamental issue – positive or negative. It is merely a passing newspaper headline, another episode in the everyday affairs of the 'bound-in-freedom' Federal Republic of Nigeria.

Biographies

FARAH AHAMED is a short fiction writer. Her stories have been published in *The Massachusetts Review, Thresholds, Kwani?, The Missing Slate* and *Out of Print* among others. She was highly commended in the 2016 London Short Story Prize and has been nominated for The Caine and The Pushcart prizes. She has been shortlisted for the SI Leeds Literary Prize, DNA/Out of Print Award, Sunderland Waterstones Award, Asian Writer Short Story Prize and Strands International Short Story.

SINDISWA BUSUKU-MATHESE was born in 1990 in Durban. She is currently based in Stellenbosch and is a PhD student at Stellenbosch University. She has recently published her first collection of poetry, titled *Loud and Yellow Laughter* and published by Botsotso. She has also published several poems in various local poetry journals such as

New Coin, *New Contrast*, *Prufrock*, *Aerodrome* and *Ons Klyntji* and has featured in the *Sol Plaatje European Union Anthology*. She was awarded second place for the 2015 Sol Plaatje European Union Award for her poem *Portrait of a Mother and Indiscretion*.

JUSTIN DINGWALL is a successful commercial photographer and contemporary artist. He's exhibited both locally and internationally – including a solo exhibition at the North West University in 2016 – and recently made the top 10 in one of Africa's most prestigious art competitions, the 2014 Absa L'atelier. Dingwall started his career in commercial photography after graduating with a BTech Cum Laude in Photography in 2004. His commercial clients include Adobe, MAC Cosmetics, Sony and Sasol. Over the last few years he's won numerous awards, including gold in the Fuji Film Awards for portraiture.

BEYERS DE VOS is a writer, journalist and editor working in Cape Town. He has completed an MA in Creative Writing at the University of Cape Town. He wrote his first novel in 2016.

DILMAN DILA is the author of a critically acclaimed collection of short stories, *A Killing in the Sun*. He has been shortlisted in several awards, including the BBC International Playwriting Competition (2014), the Commonwealth Short Story Prize (2013) and the Short Story Day Africa Prize (2013, 2014). A number of his short stories have featured in several magazines and anthologies. His films include *What Happened in Room 13* (2007) and *The Felistas Fable* (2013), which was nominated for Best First Feature at the Africa Movie Academy Awards (2014) and won four major awards at the Uganda Film Festival (2014).

AMATESIRO DORE is a 2009 alumnus of the Farafina Trust Creative Writing Workshop, former managing editor of *Vanguard Spark*, an imprint of Vanguard Newspapers, and a 2015 Fellow of the Ebedi International Writers Residency. He studied law at the Igbinedion University and the Nigerian Law School, and his works have been published in and by *Afridiaspora*, *Bakwa* magazine, Brittle Paper, Farafina, Kalahari Review, Kwani?, *Munyori Literary Journal*, *Queer Africa II*, *Saraba* magazine and elsewhere. He has won the Saraba Manuscript (Non-Fiction) Prize and the Reimagined Folktales Contest. He lives and writes in Lagos, Nigeria.

TANIA HABERLAND (formerly van Schalkwyk) is a pussy- and cock-loving poet, artist and body-worker. She won the Ingrid Jonker Prize for poetry in 2010 and is co-creator of a healing practice called Oceanic Somatics. Whether working with people or writing or creating, she is interested in ecstatic living.

JULIA HANGO is drawn to the processes of birth, death and renewal. She tries to capture what lies below the surface of society's misconceptions and stigma surrounding nudity and the female body, and the qualities of the 'unseen' that express the sense of wonder that she feels in her daily existence. Julia had three solo exhibitions in 2015 as well as one group showcase in Sweden. She was chosen to exhibit at the 2016 That Art Fair in Cape Town, South Africa.

DEAN HUTTON is a genderqueer artist interested in portraiture as co-authorship, social media as narrative, and technology as self-reflection and provocation. Currently, Dean is pursuing a Masters in Fine Art and Drama with the Institute for Creative Arts (ICA) at the University of Cape Town. Dean has worked across photography, video, social media, performance and community programmes since the late 1990s. The photograph of Dean in this series is made in collaboration with Alberta Whittle.

OTOSIRIEZE OBI-YOUNG was shortlisted for a 2016 Miles Morland Scholarship. His story, 'Mulumba', appears in *The Threepenny Review*, and his transition story, *A Tenderer Blessing*, was nominated for a Pushcart Prize in 2015. His essays appear in *Interdisciplinary Academic Essays and Brittle Paper*, where he is currently submissions editor. He has completed a collection of short stories and will soon begin a novel but is currently searching for a literary agent. He grew up in Aba and attended the University of Nigeria, Nsukka. He currently teaches English at Godfrey Okoye University, Enugu, Nigeria.

OLAKUNLE OLOGUNRO is an English language student in the University of Ilorin. He currently resides in Lagos, Nigeria, and is an alumnus of the Farafina Trust Creative Writing Workshop.

AYODELE SOGUNRO is a Nigerian writer, social entrepreneur and lawyer. He is the author of *The Wonderful Life of Senator Boniface and other Sorry Tales,* and the collection of critical essays, *Everything in Nigeria is Going to Kill You.* His widely read writings have earned him references in both local and international media, and have been published or mentioned in several Nigerian and foreign news outlets. He has been interviewed by *Ebony* magazine, AFP, France 24, BBC Africa and *The Daily Caller,* to name a few.

SARAH WAISWA is a Kenya-based freelance documentary and portrait photographer with an interest in exploring identity on the African continent, particularly the new African identity. After getting both sociology and psychology degrees and working in a corporate position for a number of years, she decided to pursue photography full time. Her desire is to illustrate the plight of various social issues on the continent in a contemporary and non-traditional way. She hopes to change the narrative on Africa by generating dialogue on developing issues as they happen. She is passionate about creating visual poetry and telling stories in the most organic and creative way possible.